PULP: A Manifesto

BY

JERROD E. BOHN

PULP: A Manifesto

BY

JERROD E. BOHN

Published by Unsolicited Press
www.unsolicitedpress.com
info@unsolicitedpress.com
Copyright © 2018 Jerrod E. Bohn
All Rights Reserved.
No part of this book may be reproduced or transmitted in any form or by any means without written permission from the publisher or author.
Unsolicited Press Books are distributed by Ingram.
Printed in the United States of America.
Attention schools and businesses: for discounted copies on large orders, please contact the publisher directly.
Cover Art: Mackenzie Solomon
Editor: S.R. Stewart; Kristen Gustafson
ISBN:978-1-947021-65-5

Thank you to the following presses where some of these poems first appeared.

Philadelphia Review of Books—Chokehold 2.0 (May 2015)
Yellow Chair Review—True Bromance (May 2015)
After the Pause—"Family Sitcom" (June 2015)
Vilas Avenue—Back to the Future (August/September 2015)
Belletrist Magazine—Sex in the Time of Fucking (February 2017)
Sediments—Farm to Fuck (February 2017)

PULP: A Manifesto

I

Let's play hopscotch over your pill-bottles. I don't care if you're menstruating. That loose little one in the corner needs screwed, or a table with three legs will have to do. Swill-bucket; you read contemporary poets by the fish ton. The "Voice of My Generation's" face tattooed on your face, & that scares me because once in Mexico I dreamed I was this black kid named Larry Lazarus. He wanted to break the Voice's glasses, the Voice who orated every proto-millennial's Sunday morning jazz & shizzle. Privilege is knowingly eating the last butterscotch sea salt caramel one last time. That's why Larry, a captive audience, wanted to punch the Voice in the larynx, which would have lost us another generation. Declares Larry,

Belts, garters, thigh-high
fishnets my fingers cant
swim out of, a blue-
eyed citizen w/ a discernible face

she said I got a switch
inked below my ribcage

"American slavery is a state of mind"—the Voice, high school Lincoln-Douglas Debate Event, Lawrence High School, Kansas (the state in which the Voice & I became acquainted). Everyone Sharpied this into their notes except Larry, who knew what being sealed in a cave felt like, the insurgent prescription of an old Southern spiritual—it's rocking time in them old cotton BVDs hoping Colin Kaepernick will stand up this time because America loves an eloquent sports cliché to keep running 'em between the lines. Larry Lazarus, come to sing our resurrection.

*

Practice kneeling, Larry
Lazarus is the hero
is also Colin Kaepernick

(& the Voice found static within
too much silence
sings Larry:

"America is a slave state"

Trump would look better in tights teaching a five-year-old to pirouette, to skirt the bushes that he's inherited his voice from. If a national election ever comes down to one vote, maybe I'll cast it. He's playing the presidency & all the ducks have dollar bill heads. My Nintendo zapper's jammed & spraying two-party rhetoric, that asshole hunting dog is laughing at me & I can't look at two wrecked towers & know they ever stood—

Rampage: two monsters
bashing buildings
tusks & tails a video game—

Colin Kaepernick discoursing
but we love our athletes dumb
& gracious, "better beer
Larry again, bro"
Believe that all life is a pixel. LL loves Ariana. LL's way too into sex. To save money, Ariana outsourced her see-through yoga pants to some sexless child, sewing to support the gods we imported, transgendered to have a realpolitik facial scar, a stretchy star underneath the right cheek.

Larry, sing.

*

Paranoid that "literally" may be the post-person condition. Moved beyond mustache-level irony to "what's that dirt-squirrel under your nose *really* mean?" Listened to another NPR poet read in a smug, "is it coffee or whiskey or hot anal lube" kind of way. A Faust, whose market poetry feels formed where all the pinups wear black Ray-Ban pasties. A Faust, whose market voice is two-tenths barroom scribble & the rest a ham sandwich he sold in the breakroom at Pitchfork.com. Hipsterdom is the best thing to happen to America because aren't I tired of re-inventing the Western snapshirt? I'm just another cigarette a cowboy poet tries to bum in a snowstorm. AWP Chicago. Larry Lazarus, metaphorically.

"You're such a cute little girl writing your cute little girl poems"—to my classmate, who idolized him, said a former U.S. Poet Laureate, who I could say resembles a scraggly, squat, well-known fantasy character, but that's a cheap shot, like throwing a lame duck pass to a sideline reporter & hoping he doesn't intercept the speech.

What is it with appearances, the superficial scruff around the poet's chin, or the overly applied eyeliner, the thick hide of a knee-high boot? The artificial turf is a surface. The burn section is a surface. The gospel singers are surface. Marrow in the mouth, Larry tells her, that's texture:

I enjoyed waking up with you
covers retaining last night's
voice—this postgame
preluded by a pillow

smothered too many books
read too many pressings

*

MASTER OF THE FLYING GUILLOTINE

Crane-kick: dogma
that each violence must be art-
fully named

poet as warrior
as bawd goating
around until clamoring
for a butting of heads
some pretty name
worth mating over

animal noises exacting
martial faith

stylized fighting
to cleave skulls

to dance steps
metered, clambering.

*

The Ariana Principle → The Ariana Solution, reasons Larry

*

Self-referencing a convex mirror, turns out she had two lilies after all, her bridesmaids all asleep in the bungalow. She played a part-time chef who inspired an axe-murdering chanteuse & this is how transparent all Billy Collins's poems are, perhaps too easy a poet to dislike. I had to try harder to hate Frost. But back to these flower girls asleep in the blue snow. I remember reading Vikings were really just nice guys, pick up your bar tab, then blood-eagle. The principle is this: the poem's political dimension plays Candyland like a pampered baby. All entrance, the poem asks no exiting.

*

Ways of Seeing

I spent today looking through windows.
The chalk outline blew away to reveal

grids of a previous architecture. Wind
stalled. I don't remember landscapes

distinct portraits of an invisible woman
gendered to become her mouth's

crisis. A green city rose
in her throat. I don't believe there was

wind. I passed time plucking petals
from trees. The previous architecture

resembled an English garden where a poet
stood with a laurel & a passing breeze

through him. The woman wanted to speak
but she lacked a face. She is only a hand.

*

I'm skeptical of a poem that is too polished, like going to hear live music only to have the band sound just like the album. Feeling ripped off when you know what's going to happen next. The concert's energy is in pops & accidental feedback, the banter between the crowd & band members. Band bantering among itself. A broken string.

Or at a restaurant & unexpectedly smiling at finding a mushroom in my dish that doesn't feature them, a juicy, earthy mistake among eggplant, basil, bits of bamboo. The shitty catastrophe of Billy Collins's poem "Introduction to Poetry" is that it names itself into the very thing that it is. Billy Collins, the Original Hipster, & the irony that the young avant-garde hate the OH
while dishing up the same frozen, prepackaged Applebee's poems.

Note to a vegan writer: replacing chicken wings with seitan stopped being transgressive, nor ever actually was.

*

Reality Bites

The work is manifest before
its un-Maker

a toenail clipping falling into a web
gives the spider pause.

This isn't to say hangnails
become less annoying,

or Sunday funnies replaced by furniture ads
cause more vexation than cold
coughing fits. Unity

at once turns
the un-Maker's song, heard

in compulsive finger's
chewing patterns inward.

We have searched
sports pages to browse
our bloopers, laughing to ignore
our thumb's bloody spaces
stumped by crosswords

unwove & unwove until boxes wove themselves in
light bulbs burnt out, we could scarcely hear

dull twangs, tensile strand—
in this time of how many trumps
the wound's trimming passes as a small meal

we lol ourselves to sleep on the absurd
rows & letters of a tweeted bed.

*

Attended a poetry reading & what to hashtag it. Burroughs's *Naked Lunch* & original poems & stories with no relation to junk other than the idea being conceived as a launch event for a Dutch beer, also without relation to junk. The crisis: I can't drink with another poet without comparing. Some of them are even my friends.

An open mic is a queue of one, like looking in the mirror at anything but your own gaze, which is always male, subordinating you to your reflection's convex object-space.

I cringed when I read the contributor's copy because why am I here? A half dozen blocks away there's a donut shop that donates its holes. Is it whoring if you're never on the receiving end?

My computer's updating. Its status: "Setting Up a Few More Things." It knows most of us won't understand the specifics. Best to speak in ambiguities. Like every love poem I've ever written can end on the odd or even pulled petal depending on what the one holding the daisy wants to believe.

Today, Seattle is sunless. An entire empire reduced to wearing bougainvillea shorts. If the open mic is an open bar, half of us would be dead. That's why I give my vote to holding the AWP Conference in Las Vegas. Even in

Lawrence, KS hippie kids passed out on Burroughs's lawn, waking up cold & confused with their lunch money jangling in their pockets & absolutely no idea that horizon is synonymous with home.

*

If the AWP Conference were ever held in Las Vegas, Larry Lazarus would outlive us all.

*

One night, shooting pool with an MFA colleague, we got into a game for money with some drunk we took to be a hustler. After losing multiple rounds of drinks, he admitted he was a writer. He carried a duct-taped backpack. He looked like he didn't have much skin. Inside the backpack, he had stacks of manuscripts he carried for Tuesday nights in July when he ran into two other writers who often told people they were teachers but just happened to let the "p" word slip. Two writers who didn't know why they were ashamed to confess themselves, or was it just easier not to say? When you have to answer, "who's your favorite poet?" and you end up feeling hipster because it isn't God, Shakespeare, or Rumi. And then you have to hear, "you should read Jimmy Carter or Maya Angelou," and you walk away relieved that they didn't say Billy Collins.

But this guy was proud to admit he's a poet, even offered both of us bracket-clipped copies of his complete manuscript. He knew we absorbed the profound boredom of this moment when he began telling us of his wife & kids & two weeks on the road to distribute that very document to two guys in a bar who just wanted cigarettes, cold beer, & warm pockets because tomorrow would only bring them the quietude of morning coffee & self-loathing.

Here was this guy with his lineated genitals out on the table begging us to take a gander, & I couldn't bring myself to look in the mirror later that night & it was several months before I thought about how his manuscript was 65 copies of the same poem.

*

This Peace, This Wharf

In Seattle no one walks
where there aren't gulls

waves sometimes gather
in town & thereafter
an abundance of discarded crab shells

I've never been to BC
though I've heard drinking songs
too recent to be memory

She came home today & had the coffee poured
1/3 hot water as to her preferred taste
for peculiar hand-drawn baths I have
little to speculate

Meandered down to the gulf
so broke
I can't make a whole sand dollar

In times of intense narration
as in sailing I dreamed
Seattle at war w/ its own current

which of course is its inability to rid its shores
of squawking

She came home today where the key wasn't
under the rock because I'd gone
running, the Sound
distant, flat

I finally visited Vancouver & drank
until I forgot that once I swam
myself to exile
excrement clinging so close
to every foot-trodden
stone or sand.

*

After a reading, a poet in a bar bathroom thought he walked in on me getting ready to go down on Larry

Lazarus. Even though I insisted I was straight, the man ran his hands across Larry's abs & said, "how can you pass this up?" Frankly, I didn't know.

*

Later on, some of that poet's groupies asked me to score them some blow.

*

OLD YELLER

Of consequence, a dying dog
licking the day's last sunshine
because it will return his shadow
wheezing across the lawn

in sunbaked worms a stalled calendar
our footsteps, too, hot on cement
hating the weather because it's all we talk about
worrying we'll have to put him down

returned to when the oak swing
was not the kind of object
you could overthink to destroy

this expected line break, executed
to absolve him of his shame
barking at the tire & eating
his own shit—

tomorrow a slight chance of no rain.

*

Happy Hour (@ the Post-Person Bar & Grill)

Past noon, to have a complete lunch
bread/meat/cheese & if one's lucky
dill pickle's company

she said she'd meet me here at 3
these pints will not drink themselves
afternoon's angrier after
a downpour

half price umbrella drinks to warm the techies
who tip lousy & demand
slightest sexual interludes

sweat on my beer glass, 5
fingers tapping checkered cloth

I'll give her until half past 4.

*

If she found out I stayed awake thinking about ex-lovers would she still fall asleep? That my tearing at the sheets has nothing to do with warmth, instead the heat of a mythologized summer, or a surprise homecoming, or a deliberate touch on an accidentally shared stair? So easy to remember reaching under a skirt, leaving potatoes to boil, volume lifting curtains off screens. Smelling so musky neighborhood dogs pant behind windows on our evening walk. Forgetting the empty bottles on the porch, her playing footsy under the table with my best friend while I thought of future bar girls who left smoke & mascara on my pillow. An oblivious husband thinking it odd that the dog didn't bark at me.

I am aware of factual fictioning. She rolls over & the yawn in her eyes is asking. When I sleep on my back I stop breathing. I am aware of manufacturing authenticity. With no kiss, she moves me onto my side.

*

Sex in the Time of Fucking

This pulp, this metapoetry, this
scripture speaking for collective
that singular summer chopping vegetables
how we left them
scattered near the stove. Didn't bother

to fully undress. When you're in love
anywhere's a bed. Windows
prove wall's limits
are artificial. Swallowed

a small voice when we got up, forgetful
of our hunger. No moral
implied by filling the belly

or speaking about what's behind
our mesh screens. Neighbor's

lit window. Dogs
howling for our meal's compost

spread across the kitchen
island our breathing
as if to no one.

*

THUG LIFE

You concealed the act
framed as if a song was caged
in your throat's depth, a rustled
victim rattled all along

not knowing your hushed voice. My hand
raised to draw hot water
to scald conciliatory
silence over morning newspapers.

The surge blew out kerosene
its breath to relight the hearth

wood gathering drizzle. A slow heat
fog on the glass's inside
builds between notes
I knew you stared through
to our other room.

*

The poem is anything but a gift. The poem is an insipid disease. Burrowing its way under its reader's skin, the poem spreads like a star burst. Once contracted, symptoms include disorientation, loss of linear time, heightened sensory awareness, visceral tingling, a detaching of signifier from signified, echolalia, glossolalia, euphony, cacophony, a violent severance from perceived reality, a perception as though being in an infinite room, euphoria, & descent. The poem is highly contagious & can be transmitted through breath, touch, & always sexually. The poem often invites itself in. If you've had the poem once, you can expect flare-ups even when the symptoms appear to recede. These will occur at irregular & inopportune times, like when you're out to dinner & become obsessed with a freckle on your lover's forearm because an entire cosmogony appears there. You can't rest until you've named every species of bird. If you suspect you have the poem, avoiding contact with others will only result in the creation of nearly 800 hand-bound chapbooks. So live your life as normal, knowing it's never been. The poem is the proverbial gift that gives.

*

Future Music

Resigned to pluck guitars
of infinite matter, chords
as an old musician reclines
in an old chair, witnessing
old names he gave. His craft
notched into fingertips,
latticework smell
after rain. The ground

marches an ancient accordance
& he is aware of deep song

crisscrossing the verdant grid.
Never one for tuning
save rhythmic

pastimes of breath
distant voicing

this is nowhere
their meanings.

*

Post-Personing (for Larry Lazarus)

A light mechanism, belief
that one's personal rituals

allegorize, that prayer too
is universal, is

decay. The communion
lines' ritual is its hinge—

a circle on a tongue
that will encircle a body

given no shape. Its daily magic
readying to leave

an imagined stasis springing
always toward return.

*

The night after the election, I walked behind the backstop. There was nothing to say. The pitcher had thrown well, struck out many, walked few. She'd done what was asked. Never questioned the signs or hot-dogged it against a dangerous hitter. If the game plan were a living entity, she would have chopped its head clean off.

I kicked a peanut shell out of my path. What to say to Larry? Sometimes the decapitated creature stands back up. Sometimes you hold it by the throat, but it still leads you. Sometimes when you clear all the dirt off you just don't know trace

II

This Peace, This Wharf 2.0

Tonight, let's trample sandcastles
kick broken shells back to sea

the moon's donned its armor,
tired of being naked
sitting here next to you, our toes
digging in foam. Stars
are principle form, liquid

an air between our lips gasping
that lit space might soon
go blank of time

blank of all we know. Alone
far from the now-sleeping gulls
tides seeming to carry

as they run along the beach to reset
each pebble. With luck
we won't need this blanket
will stand with our backs

to water, skin bared to shore
now blurred into silver shadow
until our hair scrapes sky
in haste to cover our bare heads
fully aware of the hour.

*

Poem-time operates through several intellectual & visceral exchanges, some concurrent so as to appear bonded, others in succession so as to imply causality; to mistake them as such suggests linearity. Exchanges within the poem's dialogic space are neither simultaneous nor serial; rather, these energy transfers occur always on their own scales. Poem-time exudes a sense of always arriving & departing. In its infinitude, poem-time situates itself in the present, much like an infinite network, a repeating room that despite its seeming sameness generates new random encounters.

In early scrolling RPGs & dungeon crawlers, video game players often encounter a forest (in *The Legend of Zelda*, this is referred to as "The Lost Woods") or a section of a cave or fortress that repeats. After dispatching some slimes or wizard vampires, the hero/adventure party traverses to the edge of the screen that coincides with a cardinal direction. A brief pause. The screen shifts & reconstructs itself. The adventurers arrive at their point of departure.

The 8-bit blobs designating brown trees or blue brick walls lineate a poem. Our heroes navigate the verses. Once they have accessed the infinity maze, to retrace their steps only leads them deeper into the void. There is no forward or backward. There is only the room.

*

Advice to Link on (Re)Entering The Lost Woods

Name the first creature you see
the first name that comes to your tongue

its name the same as it is now, pronounced
as though forgotten, as if syllables
are unfamiliar yet known

the imagination's work is erasing

whole thickets
so that each new step brings regrowth
things already called

foreign to the ear though sound
takes you back to the river

a fairy, perhaps, singing

to chase that echo into the heart of it
become lost among roots
you know so well

reacquainted with branch & bramble
leave then knowing nothing
will surprise you—she has sung of this

& your throat evolves
the trunk's previous rungs.
*

However, to suggest the room is the same isn't always accurate. Thanks to random encounter algorithms, new monsters & treasures await. The boundaries do not shift; the energies within are in perpetual flux.

Sensing the infinity maze's frustration to a largely young male audience influenced by their parents' capitalist values, video game design pioneers made the market-saving move to offer escape. By following a pattern of sequential movements ("go north, west, south, west"), the brave hero "solves" the riddle to emerge to a fresh location of conquest. To linger in the maze, lacking any sense of forward movement, unnerves the body/mind conditioned by mono-directional time. Designers knew the necessity to establish an exit to comfort the questers in pursuit of profit & reward. There had to be a way out. In a market system, entering requires leaving.

*

Legend of Drunken Master

Stayed up all night learning the art
of how the moth practices its fight
evading cat-claws to come to rest
on a beacon—oops

that's one of those blue electric lamps
should have drank one less beer. There's knowledge
to unlock, so leave me studying
why the light draws us
when we know it will drown us

lessons here so ancient that we must
be serious dumbasses for not figuring it out

or born at the wrong time, lacking
a long enough Fu Manchu falling over our jawlines

blow out candles. My mistake
was lighting it. I should go instead
to where wings are wound in a web
spider so close its reflection

bobs up & down
eight intent eyes on its struggle.

*

I'm now certain that Spenser's "Bower of Bliss" is a prototype of the infinity maze (as is, perhaps, Circe's island), albeit one with far more lure than encountered in a typical dungeon crawler. Rife with sensual, often erotic energy, Spenser created a space that anyone would want to incessantly explore, save the temperate knight Guyon, who must destroy it so that Spenser (a proto-capitalist) can continue his epic goal of winning his "Faerie Queene's" fiscal patronage. [SIDENOTE—I'm convinced Spenser's unfinished poem is just waiting for someone to transform it into a video game and/or movie franchise. Heterosexual teenage boys would lose their shit seeing the "Bower of Bliss" on the big screen].

Unlike those initial RPGs, a true poem does not offer release by mastering a code (or, in the case of Spenser, hacking the entire world to smithereens), although too many educators still approach the teaching of poetry (both reading & writing) in this way. We find ourselves leaving but always returning to the same place, although here fresh energy exchanges wait, guaranteeing that perpetual, purposeless motion persists.

Perhaps game designers haven't tapped Spenser's "Bower of Bliss," because, like Spenser, they've discovered that to make the infinity maze too sexy is simply a bad business plan. A good poem is like hitting pause-reset time & time again.

*

CHOKEHOLD

What given inheritances
birth the tongue's limit

full knowable light, air
that cannot be denied
hunger, water, sleep
a fire around
which people gather, measured
by their last belonging

while idiot meals maintain
w/ their exclusion
static bellies

the law has somewhere enabled
itself as authority

bankrupt carrier pigeons
ride the Jetstream
away from windowless

maternity wards.

*

The micro-drama of sports captivates the American attention. We don't have to think—can multitask & still feel the subtle nuance projected by six angles of vision in varying levels of real-time motion. By the time we dissect the previous play, the action has moved forward. Sport is an always-present bounded by a beginning & end. A mistake may manifest as afterthought or project some later time into crisis. Fluidity is allowed only between whistles & butt slaps. Do not interpret halftime as caesura.

I don't think it's wise for writers to shun sports any more than sports fans to shun the arts. But sports are not poetic, & we err in thinking them metaphors for life or war. Both are imagined pleasures. Both bodies—or bodied. However, sports' poetic achievement is that it makes no claim on the attention outside of time, the clock's tick & if you look away, the play won't let you come back, even as painfully you are aware that you're older, searching the replay, later the box score one last time.

*

Atrocity Encyclopedia

You forget to count minutes
notched in bellies
gone hollow, ever-glow inviting

some to take pictures, some
to drop change

streets as corridors
for passengers as vehicles

America is a diner
serving the last sloppy joe
on Route 66

hills alive with the sound
of more traffic

when human becomes capital
what passes for art, minds
money-on-paper
only keep mouths gagged

body twitching
to tap at nothing

while winter repeats
deep silence, scarcely
a patch of wet snow.

*

Larry's resemblance to an aesthetic is accidental.

A partially integrated field—a panoply of grass—there's a bee in your bloomers & baby it's got back.

Poetry is making familiar that which has become so familiar that it has been forgotten.

*

Today, I heard news of war. I was inside looking at pictures of designer cupcakes frosted to look like succulents—*Are they dry or moist?*—when shrapnel appeared like accidental pornography in a company sales meeting, only the violence looked intentional—that dildo really meant to be inside there. Despite not hearing about war for three hours, I knew we still engaged our enemies. When I walk outside, even inanimate objects, like bus booths, keep their senses on what waits. The authorities want your trust, so every once in a while they'll harass someone whose face presupposes the new danger.

Most days, I go around pointing a gun to my head, so people won't talk to me about war, though the barrel is my finger & the chamber is empty because really I just want someone's time. I don't want to discuss if calling a burrito shop "Illegal Pete's" is culturally insensitive, if the presence of six armed officers is necessary to restrain the intellectual pirate— if I believe my vote will ever matter.

My hand's getting tired because war won't let it rest. If it isn't the fifth bullet, the Newsfeed cases the sixth & soon I won't be able to hold anyone's gaze. I'm tired wherever I go, from the semi-automatic fire of public school standardized testing to the guy with the Jesus sign above I-5, whose peace wave might be a piece aimed for my blind spot. While the man stuck it to me, I fell asleep, our eyes locked for a moment over my shoulder.

*

alienation → the modern condition
fracture → the postmodern condition
paranoia, fear, apathy → the post-person condition

*

Twice this week, the man holding the Jesus sign has almost stopped my vehicle on the interstate. He calls himself (or his project, that post-person extension of self) "God Bridge." Standing in the middle of bridges spanning busy sections of the Pacific Northwest's I-5, "Brother Paul" (as he is referred to by fans on his Facebook page) has been using his handcrafted Christian billboards to bestow blessings on motorists since April 2010 (the date of his 1st "God Bridge" selfie). In eight years of hovering above traffic with captive drivers in his Biblical crosshairs, I wonder how many others he's almost made shit themselves.

My fear of overpass bridge snipers has no clear antecedent. Growing up, I watched news stories about interstate gunners in Ohio & Florida & I saw the arrest of the DC snipers unfold on CNN. As I research these shooters now, I realize that their case circumstances didn't create my fear. Nor do I have any subconscious anxiety about religious fanatics, aside from not wanting to be interrupted while drinking coffee on a café patio, told my reading of poetry is "womanly" & then asked if I want to talk about God's "manly" but platonic love.

Moreover, when I'm going over a bridge, I don't sweat a bullet entering my brain (probably due to the presence of guardrails or inches-thick cement blocking my car from those below). The paranoia is unique to death from above.

So far, I haven't floored the brakes, spun my tires so they leave visible marks & a smokescreen not even the William Tell of firearms could hit a target through. Moreover, the fear hasn't caused me to stop driving because I don't cringe at every mile marker with an overpass. The thought of seeing my front windshield snowflake before the bullet lodges in my cranium seems to occur randomly (August 2013 near Denver, Colorado—overpass bridge w/ a pedestrian walkway, a woman hovering over the freeway filmed by a movie crew; July 2014 in Western Kansas—overpass bridge w/ orange construction cones, no sign of workers or heavy equipment; October 2014 outside of Portland, Oregon—"Brother Paul" aka "God Bridge").

In such instances, my shoulders feel compressed against my ears. I have trouble breathing. But the sweat that soaks through the sides of my shirts is what lingers.

*

BIGOREXIA

My gift to you has always been hatred
looking in the mirror

at my matchstick arms, distended
belly, thick skull obese
with some idea I'll never write

two nouns
verbing the in/between

until self digests
thought. We blame

curry for making us surly
alcohol for not being water

stone or bed. Take this bread
& tattoo it

let it gestate until words make us
victims, until victims
bodies that can't sense the doings
undone by giving

why you might crave this
two shits for how
you carry it with you, attempt
its return

dysmorphic whether or not
you can hunger.

*

Here's another scenario: I'm walking at night on a public university campus. Most of the courses have concluded. Except for the janitors, the over-caffeinated engineers, & the MFA workshoppers, salivating to start meeting their nightly booze quotas, the buildings are empty. I lock the office that I, as an adjunct, share with three others. My thoughts measure my steps. Tonight, they are on the student in my 8 a.m. literature class who has started attending again after nearly a month.

Two weeks into the semester, the student disappeared for the first time. When he returned, he told me he'd been taking care of his brother who got mugged walking home from school. His brother ended up in the hospital with a concussion & some broken ribs but without the tennis shoes he'd worn when he left home that morning. My student said he was going to kill them. I excused his absences. When he came back this time, he didn't have a reason.

I told him I'd have to fail him. He said he wanted to finish the course "out of respect for me." This reverent demonstration involved him arriving daily 5-10 minutes late in his dirt-streaked black trench coat. He would sit in the back of the room with his arms crossed, his mouth drawn into the half-grimace one gets as a boy before lighting the firecracker that demolishes the anthill or tossing a live cat into a furnace. He (we) never spoke again. His eyes, often red & swollen, remained fixated on me the whole time.

As my bike lock unclicks, I look over my shoulder. The chilly, late fall wind blows browning leaves across the sidewalk. My student isn't there; that's not the scenario.

This is the scenario: I'm living in Seattle, teaching a 6 a.m. yoga class in the gritty U district. About a half hour prior, the neighborhood's addicts started coming down. Most roam for an awning to sleep under; a few seek their next fix.

I arrive alone, at least 15 minutes before my students begin to show up. As I spin the 4th digit on the lock box into place & begin to retrieve the key, I hear a click.

Down the street, there's a bridge. Two headlights break through the oppressive drizzle. They appear suspended through the slits in the safety rail.

The key fits into place, turns the locking mechanism. Moisture kicked up by the tires resettles. I go inside.

*

True Bromance (For Victoria W.)

I'm just another guy
dreaming for a Transamerica

an ordinary man's man wearing plaid snap shirts

who wants sparkling mineral water
when the vending machine only has
non-bubbly artisanal water, so I take my change, use it
to write a poem, still dreaming

to be cat-called from the street
to play footsie under a table
with my best friend's straight boyfriend

the editorial advice: "show them you're just a dude
writing dude poems"

                                              he used to text me
                                              pictures of his cock
                                              called it accidental

America is so *dude*
so bro let's buy another craft beer & end tonight
staring at each other before a street sign
not sure if we want to fuck or fight
where our walks diverge

                                              one time you told me

> two androgynes were in the alley
> one on knees, one grabbing head
> you weren't sure you just

perform the part that preserves you
long enough
to unlock your front door.

*

America is a public disturbed by ambiguity. Even those who claim to be subversive do so only if the boundaries are clear. Condition that: the homosexual is cisgendered. Condition that: the animal I won't eat could still be my pet. Condition that: Colin Kaepernick never plays football again. Condition that: our president was an articulate black man. Condition that: Larry

Is. With such conditionals, it's no wonder America hates poetry that "doesn't mean." By "doesn't mean" I refer to those poems that recognize ambiguity as an essential feature of poetry. The popularity of Billy Collins is that he is not a poet. Applying this definition, it's challenging to find one example of poetry in *The New Yorker* or assert that the United States has ever had a poet laureate. Robert Frost is an occasional poet. So is Ginsberg. Dickinson always was.

Once, I received the following feedback from a poetry editor I'll call Jim. I sent poetry to Jim's magazine, which I'll call *Myopia* (SIDENOTE: party game: is it a craft beer or a literary journal? Let's try it. Mountain Standard. Smoking Glue Gun. Space Ghost. Double Wide. If you chose *Smoking Glue Gun*, make all your friends drink & fuck it, drink with them). Anyhow, Jim was kind enough to send me a personalized rejection (SIDENOTE: rejoinder: I'm grateful for Jim's time. Individualized responses to literary journal submissions are rare given the shortage of human capital to critique. That Jim sent me anything is appreciated despite his disconcerting message).

Jim writes, "You have a gift for imagery in these poems, but after reading them several times, I can't make any sense of them. I suggest using your talent for language and description to create something readers can relate to, something like, 'a guy really wants a Coke, but when he goes to the office vending machine all he discovers is

7-Up.' You know, something that says to the audience, *I'm just an ordinary guy who happens to write poems."*

What Jim advises isn't writing poetry. Jim, who I risk transforming into the American EveryReader (SIDENOTE: assertion of fact: fuck it, Jim is the American EveryReader), wants his poetry to have a stable meaning. He needs the guy in the office to unquestionably feel unrequited thirst because to entertain any alternate readings would complicate the metaphor or worse, bring Jim's worldview into a kind of ambiguity where ordinary guys maybe don't write poetry. They shuck oysters & form crab cakes. They kiss their cousins as little boys & wait for mommy to leave so they can raid her closet.

As categories of tolerance continue to expand, so do their constraints. What we perceive to be transgressive just shifts or reasserts new, stable fields of meaning. Until American readers adopt definitions that truly allow for ambiguity and slippage, what reallyconstitutes poetry (SIDENOTE: definition: night's bluest moment) will continue as marginalized when confronted by non-shifting interpretations that accompany a so-called erosion of norms.

*

OATH IS A POINT WE'RE SETTLING ON

Twenty degrees off magnetic north
foxes mouse & splatter snow

                      over a checkered tablecloth
                      she looks at me, the tea-light
                      turns the carnation's shadow
            plastic. I've heard the pho here is good

Today a friend texted me about a genocide. "Ethic cleansing," as autocorrected. A paw print in colonial drift. The Christian missionaries knew the best method of assimilation is through the bleaching of the tongue

                when she spoke she almost always fidgeted
                            biting off her hangnails

a fox is a cat in a red jacket

more to cardinal directions than a question of whose god

the flakes won't melt, though breath
makes of inactivity an act

My friend & I debated the death toll when tragic becomes statistic. By altering the larynx you've rearranged the face. We supposed it better not to have a face

a matter of ordering off the "authentic Vietnamese menu"

>   on a date, the abandoned partner
>   will always check the phone
>   until the other returns from the restroom

the fox's kill rate is 73%
jumping NE of true

I read about a tribe that only speaks in the present. They don't know the linear history of a flag

blood is on the page
& every page connects

itself to its prey.

*

TO BE AT ONCE DUST & THE WORLD ENTIRE

I think it a fundamental mistake (one rife, admittedly, with insecurity) to claim that because you are a poet you see the world with greater depth, clarity, sympathy, or understanding—the same type of error that leads the politician to enact laws that reaffirm cultural, ethnic, gender, class, and other social divisions in the guise of helping "humanity" (who he believes he knows better than they know themselves), although with arguably less disastrously felt results. Yours is simply a manner of seeing.

Today, I watched war emasculate
itself on national TV. I was
afraid, having already been
assigned a column & rank. I thought
I would fight by planting
a sapling in the sidewalk & learn
to sleep between leaves out of view
of pedestrian birds trailing flesh

> *observable: my rifle*
> *near the mail -order*
> *catalogue a hand -*
> *model taped over*
> *the flag's geopolitical*
> *mouth like a hunting*
> *trophy caricature*
> *a cartoon doe*

lights syncopated every casualty re-

spawned. Tonight the city is without
gender. I know mutilation
by its breath

> *observable: my accumulated waste*
> *a low-hanging*
> *branch a cocoon*
> *caught in an unthreading*
> *web its laborer's*
> *day song*

Poet, you do not legislate anything. You are not a cousin to primal man. There is no primal man. The antique drumming bathes itself in the masturbated blood of pure infant babble that never was. There is no reclamation notice staked over the trail to the womb. There is no womb or mythologized father with antlers & a kiss like moth flight. There is only silence. You were never born.

I kept waking. By then
the buzz diminished & I thought these things
now need names. I descended

the street depopulated until I couldn't speak
Darkness hid my tongue

> *observable: a chalk*
> *outline proportional to*
> *my present body a cement*
> *wall erasing itself*
> *in cemetery*
> *dusk a cripple*
> *rendering glyphs*

the tree

Begrudge the suit in the office elevator: he just spent sixteen hours closing an account in no one's name;

Begrudge the exec on the corporate bus: he just sold half his staff so you could eat organic, post-apocalyptic bread;

Begrudge the mother who buys her daughter a plaster bust of the beheaded princess;

Begrudge the woman who lies there like a body because
        she is made to be;
Begrudge the priest in the alb he knitted from his
        firebombed faith: his is the kingdom of have
        not's;
Begrudge the athlete, the aesthete, the acetic;
Begrudge the internet search string

I followed wind until I felt certain
rain had ceased. My home
stood exactly where it was all windows

> *observable: a card-*
> *board cutout*
> *all the clothing I owned*
> *a moth caught in*
> *cat's paws where digested*
> *my meal steaming*

intact. The channel revisited
annihilation that never was
aftermath in closed captioning

trembled through empty sockets I saw
pink & purple dahlias arranged
as I'd left them. I hungered & wanted
to get drunk to call
my ex-lover over for a celebratory fuck

dawn broke blue
outside as in

*

Two nights ago, I dreamed that two men got into a fight. I was sitting in a hotel lobby reading some sort of poetic theory when an older, professorial man became raveled in an argument with Larry Lazarus, who wore his mustache like an antique pugilist. There were some fuck yous exchanged. They started fisticuffs when the older man quoted Thoreau, sending Larry into a tizzy. "I'll kick your ass," said the elder gent & he had a fighting stance like a peacock. With one continuous motion, LL, with his majestically greased facial hair, fished out the other's eye. Milk splattered everywhere & the orb swayed back & forth like a disco ball tethered to a red rope.

I set down my book—possibly *Spring & All* but who can tell?—& took the circular pudding in my hand, noticing how it felt like cooked gnocchi in case I wanted to write this down later on a cocktail napkin, along with my phone number & a cherry stem. Using my thumb, I pushed it back into his skull. The edges went *squish* as they filled out the socket. I was on a vacation, I think, because all the drinks had toothpick umbrellas & there was something post-person about the chandeliers.

III

LOCUTION (*from* A POST-PERSON LINGUISTICS)

I woke to realize I'd always been writing the same poem.

Ariana rose to wash
vases in floodlight, peonies
outside blue-bathed

I fell asleep remembering I'd woke to write the same poem.

Or an instance of the same. I fell awake remembering.

To live outside narrative I must forget the word, all its associations, and let it return to my mouth with all its associations.

Ariana plays with dolls
though she's past
her need for stories

She likes buttercups
premature gray

behind her ear

Arose asleep to the journal I'd written in this word before though I've never used it. Only by disobeying narrative can I tell a genuine story.

I wound the ghost
day's mature clock

Could Ariana? Would Ariana? Will that the story leaves us alone. Should Ariana?

Tell ourselves, anyway, I suppose.

If I ever wake I know the exact narrative.

I used this name before.

*

Without a copy, there can be no original. The idea of "originality" only exists so long as a reproduction occurs, as in a cover song. Original thoughts cannot exist because for a thought to be original, a copy must necessarily exist.

Post-persons are reproductions of persons, but the original is unavailable. Each reproduction re-contextualizes the original, so the original can never be grasped. We cannot say, "her style is original," until we see someone copying her style; however, in post-person critiques this requirement renders any pursuit of originality fruitless. In a capitalist economy where even existence has market value, what we acknowledge as original is always already a copy.

*

We Think to Feel Again, Our Faces

This androgyny is making me
confuse dangling metaphors with real life
like how casually you slipped your thumb
into my ass last night (when I needed

to bum a ride, needed comfort

                                             backseat uncomfortable
fronting full nude reproductions
of males looking like maladies (boys will
masturbate car horns full of women), or *the closet*
always makes a good simile

                                       the like or
ass gets measured in tight denim, how we want
singularly to love our mirror, our post-
person genitalia. Take this rear
seat. The original

                                     Buick bouncing
a self-discovered desert night, wren
cresting canyon & in its song
noise that can only be already heard
thumping passenger to throat
manufactured, as in our hands, our origins.

*

When originals cannot be referenced, power groups will use reproductions to benefit the preservation of their power, industries for profit. We are convinced the reproduction has some sort of original value, but that original value is controlled and defined by the power group or marketplace. Post-persons believe a particular style or "look" is an expression of their uniqueness without recognizing that uniqueness itself is a reproduction. Self-expression is an invisible computer endlessly scanning & re-uploading facsimiles of the same thing.

*

LOCUTION 2.0 (FROM *POST-PERSON LINGUISTICS*)

Bread baskets have a way of deceiving
a crumb descended into her eye

the sequence, a banging of plates comes to mind

O your mouth's entrapment
coronet of lips—will you

pass me the gravy?

                                            butter up buttercup

your mouth's estrange—/ O
the meat is gristly

two men with a dog on the stairs
arguing snow covers hair
beneath your nose

                                        I'll make soup

she likes pairs of musical, lesbian siblings

                        we'll elope in exactly one month

break this crust & grease this hinge
eat of my body

                                              I'll draw
                                              water
                                           for feasting

out of ritual.

*

Post-personhood is a condition made possible by the ever-expanding surveillance state. Post-persons are always aware of being observed; thus, post-persons either lack interiority or, at best, have false interior lives. Interiority necessarily depends on privacy; because the surveillance state seeks to abolish privacy, the surveillance state can be thought of as attempting to eradicate interiority. Because they are always seen, post-persons do not have the solitude necessary to develop interior lives. The surveillance state perpetuates an illusion of solitude in order to mask its omnipresent & omniscient gaze. As such, the interior is automatically the exterior even if the interior seems ostensibly private.

While post-personhood affects all generations in industrialized, capitalist surveillance states, Millennials & Generation Y have a greater awareness of being incessantly surveyed & are accused of being vapid, narcissistic, & always putting themselves on display. In this sense, they are more revolutionary than the generations before them, although they have yet to escape post-personhood. The revolutionary act may be to acknowledge the illusion of interiority & broadcast all of one's whereabouts & activities through a medium the surveillance state employs. One person doing this will not undermine the state's authority; several thousand post-person transparencies will begin to erode the system because there exists nothing left to survey.

*

Triggering Town

Persons of color are more likely to be
disproportionately killed in shooting

simulations where white executives
fire Nintendo zappers at subordinates—

I drank too much one night
& wore your father's face, your English

teacher's hand inside your thigh
fleshy bruise on an apple. Accused

of silencing the female voice by my teacher
who fucked his students, creepy

the best sex I ever had mimicked
US military war scenarios

or this talk about forcibly inserting
my fantasy football lineup

makes me ashamed to have
dissected how much I enjoyed

two boys in woodshop
who beat my forearm purple

every day they wore the same Megadeth tees
I mocked them through sawdust

wincing like an aborted brother.

*

Sometimes Larry Lazarus stands up & bugles as if he had a father. I used to have antlers that I whittled to pencil points. No, not to write his name with but as if to bleed.

The pact in question like the unity of an ancestorless child.

> on the desert highway, sharpened
> sense of smell. Agate
> quartz shells preserved
> fingerbone. A man of presence
> is he even there? Moon is
> asphalt because I remember it. Eons-old
> canyons because tomorrow they are

Now clomping his hooves like his ejaculate meant something. Larry didn't know he was a son. He had a son. He will have a son.

> the man of presence has & have, is none.

*

Elephant Man (for Russell Crowe, anti-circumcision advocate)

After gym class, your uncircumcised cock
kept incognito
under long t-shirts, or pulling
your foreskin back to look like other boys
who still joke about smegma,

the girl who wanted
to text pics of your dick
to her sister because neither'd "actually seen
an aardvark." Fetishized skin-
object another insisted felt silky

on entering, how to explain
to a summer camp kid
asking why does your wee-wee
retreat into its sock tubing

whenever you grab a wrist

angling down your pants to explain

proper handling, or father
I both love you & hate
being unable to piss next to another man

how scar tissue builds
to dull sensation when you receive
the debate—

at least Maximus is on your side
& lovelies size will always matter.

*

Triggering as reclamation of lost interiority: Because they lack interiority, post-persons often speak of triggering. Like in browsing Casual Encounters (RIP) on Craigslist, the two most common disclaimers on legitimate m4w posts are "white men only" and "please be cut (i.e. circumcised)." *Sorry, not to be racist or discriminatory; that's just what I like.* & that takes you back to the YMCA locker room. That takes you back to waking up as she framed your penis across your right thigh so she could pop off a quick photo for her sister. I can't begin to understand where it takes Larry.

This is not to deny the legitimacy of trigger-based responses; instead, to suggest triggering is often an attempt to reclaim categories of being that power mechanisms have stripped away. When the interior is vacuous, the response is to fill it. When the only referent is exterior, post-persons interiorize the external, which is often defined by the ruling class. As such, the triggering often resembles a subversive act but is instead a reclamation of a false design, like claiming to every lover that "studies show it feels better" or "uncut men last longer." Though the procedure is on the decline, the CDC still estimates that 81% of men between the ages of 14–59 are circumcised.

But this is not Larry's story. I'm not the hero of this poem.

*

3:10 TO YUMA

To be the man, to put the outlaw
on a prison train, lead
him up the gallows steps
holding his gun

to body, precaution of pedestrians
maintained, procession
all order. Steps' precision

if you wander out of line
the noose will find another
pertinent neck. To ride
into desert sunset, horse
casting a low metallic shadow

hills smoking thin-
barreled, white
looking out a Stetson's brim
Western narrative of a lone known

strumming a cedar guitar
because everyone gets named in the end.

*

If every surveillance camera became unbolted, falling from the sky like lawn darts, what would be left of post-person poetry?

*

NEGOTIATIONS (FROM *POST-PERSON LINGUISTICS*)

Listen, the blue dahlia
furnaced its face to melody,
its petals fevered
crinkly like a dried-out eyeball

& anyway her hotness made me cool
laughing as I walked my pants
because it was Holy Donut Day

at the 7-11, I smoked e-
books to feel word-power
I wanted to taste her
pink pastry. Listen

in all her blue furnishings not one
crumby cathedral

god I was beggared then, just floored
her orthorexic soprano spilling wet,
my face panting
burning fresh ejaculate
my lungs full of binary
vapor, listen—alphabet

rings dissipate out my mouth
I'm sure she'd a third leg
not man enough to stroke her
inner thigh & sing
until morning's musk fries sweet dough.

I'm telling mama
your garden's hoed, I'm never
growing home.

*

My number came up at the meat counter. I looked at the anatomy, white highways crisscrossing red sand. "Perhaps you'd care for something more exotic," the butcher said, noticing the line behind me stretched out the door to where neither of us could see. "I need to get something out of my eye," I said. The butcher nodded & when I placed a four-inch splinter on the meat case, he asked, "have you ever tasted post-person?" I thought about lying, but I didn't. A four-year old pressed her snot nose against the glass, so what kind of example? "I have a feeling you're going to love post-person," the butcher continued, already wrapping a shank. "Some people say it tastes like nothing, but I just say to them 'then you ain't really tasted post-person.'"

He handed me a package, an innocuous brown in an equally innocuous shape bearing no resemblance to sinew, guts, skin. "How should I prepare it?" The line was growing longer.

Someone coughed, though it sounded dry, unneeded. Another tapped his shoe as if to suggest *I'm important & have other places to be*. Despite having chunks of skin that weren't his own clinging to his jowls, the butcher was patient, kind. I'm sure he had a child, probably not much older than the four-year old practicing bonesaw with her fingers in the fog she created with her mouth. I knew I should leave, but I hadn't the slightest clue what to do with post-person when I got home. I reposed my question: "how do you like to fix it?"

The butcher handed me a small sliver of flesh. I took it between my index finger & thumb, surprised at its lack of form. I wasn't even sure I could see it. "Do you just eat it raw?" I asked. "That's one way," said the butcher. I tossed the post-person in my mouth. "What do you think?" I shrugged my shoulders & the butcher told me to close my eyes. By now, almost everyone in line had left to be replaced by their reproductions. I could hear fabrics scrunching & slackening, joints cracking. Once again, I was holding everyone up. "Are you getting that flavor?" the butcher wondered. I rolled the porous ball around my canines, over my molars, across my tongue. I suddenly felt invisible, an apparition hovering above the crowd. They seemed connected by some sort of thread & only became more tangled as they moved, but I just kept lifting up. The ceiling tiles couldn't even hold me. "Now you're getting it," the butcher yelled up at me. I told him I was.

*

LASCAUX

My language returned to gesture
throwing a stone against

a rock wall because I do it all
knowingly, like martyrs. I can't etch

how I feel all over your chest
as I do sometimes when you're feeling
kinky, words for livestock

so much easier to pigment.
Imagination, take us back

to this war,
stamp meat grades

on our foreheads. There is no unconditional
guarantee of shaman-hood
how many times I've wished you'd kill

with paints & dyes near the wall
sketching my silhouette

to be stricken down as I draw
my uncircumcised penis

made object, made relic.

*

ELOCUTION (FROM A *POST-PERSON LINGUISTICS*)

Everyone's mouth is an excess
of body, tongue
an exercise in detachment—

tomorrow the world will blow away
leaving only throats
excised from things once grafted to

we can finally look away

on the bus, there will be
no bus, we can no longer say

what tune carries through
our earbuds, or assert our gazes'
absence of I's.

*

Despite the boundary erosions between high & low culture, academics still insist on using a scholarly language to analyze popular texts. Through this discourse, this intellectualization of low culture, definitions re-emerge because some things are still not judged worthy of serious study. But what if it were the other way around? Can we communicate high culture using the jargon we reserve for B-movies & fan fiction? In doing so, I'm sure we would discover that all art is in some way pornography. Though we can talk about aesthetics & post-person implications of fingering a puckered asshole, at the end of the day it gives pleasure & if you overthink it, you might impose meaning. Then, you'll miss the point, which is that there are numerous nerve endings on the human anus & if properly stimulated, the entire body feels pretty fucking good.

*

Reading too many sex scenes can result in the disembodiment of sex, in seeing oneself fucking or being fucked & so beginning that minded critique whereby self-objectification prevents gratification, making the carnal comical or into a kind of pastiche, sex as parody of urges—the actors all wearing masks—this thought-out farce of tangled, untouching limbs.

*

In most pornography, the woman is aware of the camera (or told to look directly at it) because the camera is male; her looking at the lens is her submission to the masturbatory fantasies of the viewer (most likely male).

Gazing into the camera, she feels herself gazed at as object & so is made to willingly participate. Her only recourse is how she is treated, which under mechanical conditions is often as sexbot, as erotic apparatus.

Which is why when women tell me, "my body is yours, do whatever you want," I know they seldom mean this. They are aware of how I am surveying them; thus, they are not meeting me as persons because patriarchal systems have made them surveyors of themselves. Have made us post-persons.

*

Nude

Is, anatomically speaking
happy smartphone cameras
aren't shaped lick pricks, though something
two-dimensional in the lens, lips
looking like an eye
seized open, even the hairless
landscape will tell you "alidade"

has a masculine echo. The surveyor
cannot keep his shadow from entering
why her face appears constantly stuck
between object

& setting. Screen itself like skin
itself is blind. She must be thinking
ridiculousness of panties
when she hears you panting

brushstrokes of your private
search string, how even in her selfies
her outstretched arm reaches
out to stroke you behind
the ear, casually.

*

Sexbot

I am sure now that this film
is meant to keep us from approximating
actual sensations

as when we step from the cinema
our eyes slowly adjust
everyone in suburbia owns a car

& anyway why are there no theater megaplexes
in central business districts?

We'll discuss the meaning of the scene
where the androids discover they aren't
attracted to organic life after all
that sex's future is disembodiment

a whole synthetic to enact
our pleasures on

& what happens when one discovers sensation
a pang rising in the belly
excising itself from the throat
what fills it

will be the subject of sequel, sexless
looking over the grunting hero's shoulder
not reacting to his sweat
falling on forehead, between eyes
the camera zooming
until the gendered nose vanishes

pupils shift right & only sound
our audible, unified moan.

IV

I Was an MFA Program Walk-On

"The man who is unable to people his solitude is equally unable to be alone in a bustling crowd."
        —Charles Baudelaire (*Paris Spleen*)

Who else makes of the arched vertebrae a holiday?

Like babe, we're in Denver performing
our love in a bedroom that reeks of someone
renting by the week, so I'm going to stick it back there

because the Cavs are in town, because cross-
over because Lebron James, because dribble penetration,
because vacation. Our daily bread,

so yeasty they'll put us on kiss cam

how can I refuse my breath
smells like every part of you, this room
appliances once used to warm tinfoil burritos

slow motion of it, *slowmotionforme*

in the rearview your spine
a structure, keeping

patrons cathedraled, index
fingers a steeple & where is god

when you discover Thumbkin has entered your anus, O
some 5,280 feet above wheatfields
run up against flatirons, dwelling.

*

PostPerson / pōst pərs(ə)n / *noun* 1. A language construct stripped of being categories. 2. A conceptual, biological apparatus. 3. The heart as apparatus; the mind as artifact.

PostPersonhood / pōst pərs(ə)n ho͝od/ *noun* 1. A named framework-state interpellated by other named framework-states. 2. A mechanism affirmed & denied by its own insistence on categorizing its being or nonbeing.

*

If one accepts the assertion of DuBois that "all art is propaganda" & its qualification by Orwell "but not all propaganda is art," then the poet (as artist) must necessarily consider the ethical life of the poem. If oppressive regimes & institutions[1] employ art to influence life to act harmfully toward other life, those who wish to rejoice in life should take care to make sure their art always promotes unity. Moreover, they need to ensure their art runs antithetical to whatever powers seek to further separation in any guise (even if that guise appears to be the betterment of all life, when in fact it simply masks further prejudicial divisions) in any sphere.

The poem's ethical power is its erosion of categories of distinction. Whenever poetry is present, a recognition (celebration?) of sameness occurs. When you step out of your tent in night's bluest (or purplest, or blackest) moment, the alabaster moon set below the canyon wall so the horizon line is not yet visible; when you can't see the stars, those sky wounds that are beginning to scab over as morning approaches; when you have to feel your way along the trees, unsure if what you are touching is

---

[1] Indictment: I don't think capitalist societies are immune, in fact they may surpass or are on equal footing in spirit of propaganda's use & intended function

bark or boulder; when you piss; when your stream feels connected to the ground and your body like an umbilical cord holding you to the earth, you are experiencing poetry.

Still, the sun rises, or your eyes adjust to delineate shapes you accept as what they are called. You become aware of yourself, your separate genitalia, the nothingness that blurred you into everything accepted as trick or illusion. Your tent mate snores; your stomach grumbles; your throat constricts in thirst.

Ethics in poetry: to write the perfect poem would keep those who experience it just outside the tent (or somewhere indeterminate since to speak the name "tent" implies distinction), obliterating all into all. The poem's ethical paradox is that to unite it annihilates. The imperfect poem offers rebirth every time; the perfect poem is true apocalypse. Poetry confronts us with oneness but cannot keep us there because its limitations as a language act to re-establish, recreate &/or reinforce distinction. The poem brings together while instantaneously severing. If one even could write the perfect poem (I still question its possibility), the ethical dilemma would pose itself as such: "would I end illusory divisions that cause suffering knowing that to do so means I must extinguish/destroy/snuff out the universe?" The poem's ethic may well be that its perfections help us see life's common fabric, while its flaws enable us to exist.

*

EXCHANGE THEORY

Even at the coffee shop, the dollar bill is an argument—

because I have several I didn't have
to sleep outdoors under an awning
in the smoggy drizzle.

Instead, I can place one in a jar
asserting my appreciation for latte art
itself, too, a propaganda

or, I can hold onto it since the barista's in a shit mood—

either way, it crinkles, will
one day coax my wallet open.

This is such a decrepit neighborhood
to which I have no moral obligation
but because I have several
I can choose choice's illusion

like how I know drinking local
really sticks it to the man.

*

American Sniper

Every poem I try to read
puts me to sleep
not as one does growing tired
or like a sick, beloved pet

or as the muscle coming to collect
protection money, or the interrogator
who knows torture
is inventing 1,000 deaths.

No, this poem-induced sleep feels
more like old cartoons
when prey leads the hunter out of the animation cell

trees vanish, background blurs
& here somehow, trigger-
mechanisms fail, physics
fails. Prey

escapes. The hunter
goes home hungry, perhaps reading
Ted Nugent's *Kill It & Grill It*
to indulge tender masochisms.

When the lamp is turned out
a hollow growl issues
from the belly, fullness

before imagination ruptures
to wake one up empty.

*

Three years ago, I moved from a mid-sized urban area—Fort Collins, Colorado (the Choice City, a craft brew mecca, Main Street USA)—to Seattle. Because of difficulty securing housing remotely, my then-partner & I rented a two-bedroom apartment unit on the main floor of a bungalow located off a busy street in the University District (the U). Unlike the ordered, manicured open spaces of UW's campus, the U is a mishmash of cheap, ethnic eateries; cheap, sleazy bro bars; and cheap, expensive corporate retail stores. The U's high student population, with its privileged naivety, backpacks bulging with laptops & smartphones, & post-person experimentalism attracts a motley host of drug addicts, intellectual transients, and those experiencing homelessness. While encounters with this latter population were not infrequent in Fort Collins, particularly around the increasingly posh Old Town Square, they are an expected occurrence anytime someone strolls a block or more away from their home in the U.

The repeated exposure to being hit up for change causes several individual emotional responses, among them:

1) Annoyance—I face tens of thousands of dollars of student loan debt & all that separates me from panhandling outside a derelict Safeway is my occasional reliance on a loving support system;

2) Depression—I want to help, but my limited job prospects (being pigeonholed as a university adjunct, work that is treated with a miniscule amount more dignity than homelessness) for upward economic mobility leave me with little to give;

3) Shame—I exit said Safeway holding a bag of produce to cook my evening meal while trying to explain that even this six-pack of craft beer in my other hand is a necessity.

Confronted with such emotions, my responses are manifold. I could:

1) Ignore them;

2) Try to acknowledge our shared humanity without financially giving, yet walk away feeling separate because of the gulf of having and not having;

3) Surrender some occasional pocket change or offer aid in a non-monetary way, perhaps volunteering to build houses or serve at a soup kitchen.

No matter what I do, I'm still faced with visions of vagrancy each time I leave my house.

In his 1972 essay on violent images from the Vietnam War "Photographs of Agony," John Berger argues that the "double violence" of publishing graphic war pictures is that such images actually divert human outrage away from the unjust conflicts political institutions are waging in "our name." They instead make the individual feel morally culpable and/or inadequate. When considering such images, the individual either "shrugs off" the emotional response or "performs a kind of penance" by donating to a charity organization, say The Red Cross. Either way, the responsibility for atrocity is pawned off onto the individual rather than the power structures, enabling the photograph to serve (to channel Althusser) as an ISA (Ideological State Apparatus) pushing the regime's agendas forward, unchecked.

It is my belief that the US government can do something about homelessness and rampant, debilitating income inequality but chooses not to because to do so would undermine the power structure of the ruling class. Moreover, the exposure of citizens to the destitute actually benefits these power groups because such interactions result in the same effects as viewing war photographs; we shrug it off, trying to accept that our hard work has provided us a better life than those "lazy bums," or we buy a guy a $2 coffee to keep him warm on a cool, rainy Pacific NW day. Regardless, the confrontation displaces responsibility onto us, not the political system that allows & benefits from such inequalities & marginalization.

To parallel Berger's views on war photography, "the next step should be for us to acknowledge our lack of political freedom," to recognize that the affront to anyone's rights to shelter, food, & water is not on the individual (often barely struggling to make sure his/her basic needs are met) but on the political systems that are supposed to make sure all people live as people. It is against the current government's interests to completely eliminate racial, gender, sexual, economic, and other disparities because encounters with these differences actually prevent citizens from demanding true reform, instead turning citizens against one another or reducing such issues to personal spheres (SIDENOTE: addendum: responses to recent waves of racially motivated police brutality are another example, how some white Americans accuse black Americans of being "too sensitive" when real lives are at stake). Power structures encourage confrontations with inequality because they preserve the elitist interests of capitalism rather than compelling citizens to demand true reform guaranteeing the rights & equality of all. The success of Donald Trump.

*

affirmation → the modern condition
curiosity → the postmodern condition
boredom → the post-person condition

*

American Sniper 2.0

Today, I murdered the poetic bird-
object. My belly is full; I don't need
to eat. In scattershot I reduced
the bird-object to feathers. I did this

for sport, for experience
having not taken literal life
to see blood and sinew
fabricating an image. Did I feel

that I felt bad. Chattering
silent now despite in memory.
I don't want to handle flesh because I am
not hungry. The bird-object's

literal existence is smithereens.
It did not recognize impact
the point its breath stopped, its wings
torn from body, its song

coagulating in in my throat.

*

Larry, I get so hard thinking about Ariana. Then, I feel guilty because I think this is maybe what they want, a white man with semen-stained boxer-briefs masturbating a book to tears.

*

AS A CHILD, I NEVER GOT TO PLAY MORTAL KOMBAT

Which is why I threw a live cat into a furnace.

Which is why I thought pulling your hair would make you love me.

Which is why I get blackout drunk & talk about dismembering those who beat me in bar games.

Which is why I'm a pacifist.

Which is why pulling your hair only made you want to be choked & being choked only made you want to be slapped & being slapped only made you come.

Which is why my only normal sexual relationships exist with women I don't love.

Which is why my medieval Lego figures always lost their appendages.

Which is why my cat hates it when I smoke.

Which is why I posted Hallmark card poetry to the Casual Encounters section of Craigslist.

Which is why my dream-fuck is probably in this bar playing shuffleboard & getting looped on IPA.

Which is why after I'd slapped your tits & ass several times I came.

Which is why my parents allowed me to play Street Fighter.

I was always Chun-Li & the one time you asked me to slap your face I couldn't because I'd just fallen in love.

*

O Ariana, please de-
fuck me. Just
once. I promise I won't
look or touch.

*

"Yes, gender difference does affect our use of language"—Susan Howe. Again, "sexual, racial, & geographical separation are at the heart of Definition."

I want to write until it renders me sexless, verbs mutilating the anatomy until each time I name I abstract. The adjective is always gendered; to noun the thing always a privileging. Which is to use my voice, my timbre, to call across an open space where the word neuters the flesh. That we differentiate between masculine & feminine. <u>That</u> we differentiate.

Feminism as a socio-political objective must continue only so long as categories of gender erode. Then, art must overwhelm the philosophy & androgenize itself. Sappho was a hermaphrodite, as is Keats. So, too, Dickinson.

The fault of feminism or any "new masculinity" is that both construct their agendas according to a recognizable, definable, historicized penis or vagina. Only by making organs metaphors rather than actuals will we further an inclusive sexual politics.

Coleridge & Woolf viewed great minds as essentially androgynous, but their definitions might be too limiting in that they seek to synthesize the gender binary. The great mind is asexual, not in terms of carnal desire (which should be voracious) but from how one gives & receives pleasure & how one views the self. Until we are artistic castrati in the truest sense, art will continue to perform sex change operations & recast the patient in new, socially defined constructs where man/woman & male/female are distinctly performative.

Poetry must de-gender & de-sex itself to become the propaganda whereby sexual politics no longer dictate

the exclusivity of physical & personality characteristics
to either a MF or MW pole.

*

INFAMOUS BAD LANGUAGES

All begin with father
because I love you dad & what I'm about to write
has no bearing on you as patriarch

some things I learned
while getting head, like teeth hurt

& it's not like on Pornhub
when she pukes I think
maybe it's me, my lack of being
financially independent at 39
or not being floored by contemporary poetry

ever, really, even my yoga
has become routine, I make love
as if before there was even undressing
my body walked down to the corner store

to buy smokes except there's nowhere to light up
every heterosexual bed hints of children.

Dad, I wish you were holding me
because I'm tired of loving

only to find that like the last book I read
my sex life needs editing

the best carry-out in town burnt my drunken noodle
& if I can keep it hard for the next six minutes
she won't act so disappointed
when I can't come. When it's quiet

I hear you singing
still populating the whole wide world
falling asleep in your hands.

*

Dandelions

If I felt in control, there might be another force
to pluck the stem, leaves

& then I see it's real, the feral daisy,
I mean the weed. Did I mean decorative
like garden gnome or those plastic

trolls with poofy neon hair & no pants
nicest inorganic ass I've ever seen

belonged to my father's riding lawn mower.

But while we're on the topic of subjugation
let's agree that "everyone works for free"

is a work in progress, is what's done
to define the face not by the labor it bears
but that it bears labor, an engine
pulling up, for food, its roots.

*

The Coup's Boots Riley might be the most entertaining & talented poet writing today. *The poem as political apparatus.* The poem does not exert subversion, does not strain against the boundaries of language. The poem circumcises the word. The work of poetry: a message of solidarity in rapt pleasure. An ever-presence. A clarion in the hypnotic dirge-march pinpointing beginning & end. Discovering that the nail in the tooth extends the tooth's range. To use the tooth as ideology & ideology always as presence.

The demonstrative mnemonic meditates on a new vowel; the always forgotten-ness of the poem is the reminder of just then. A blueprint frames the house completely, but lacks the context of what's within.

Any poet the mainstream adopts serves the mainstream, reinforces the co-opting of language to sedate, to alienate, to bind if & was. The poem is intrinsically political, & if the poet doesn't recognize this power, the power will control the function.

If the poem can be historicized, the effect is justifying the ruling class. If the poem can be futurized, its effect is preserving the ruling class. If the poem cannot be felt, the poem will not elicit action. *The poem as physic.*

The genius of Boots Riley is in verbalizing the visceral. A language that propels the body in motion is a poetics of revolution, of change—an inertial poetry that can resist the powers aligned against it. If you liberate the body from the previous action & the next action what results is dancing; if you liberate the tongue from all referents the result is presence. An exploitative system relies on past & future. Anyone who ever felt the Pentecostal flame on his or her lips swayed his or her hips (Larry Lazarus!).

To move body, to move mind, to move. Motion perpetual. The suspension & extension in IS.

*

WHY MANDATE ECONOMIC EQUALITY WHEN I HAVE SUCH GOOD LUCK FINDING MONEY

Aspen leaf near
gutter. Walgreen's

inside the ATM. Poor
mother. Her baby
carrots premature,
hungering. $6

buys me a beer. Tomorrow
I'll eat the plastic's

compost, whole.

*

They Say the Division of Man Is His Labor

If I manufactured an animal, I'd call it a pentalope from penta, meaning five; & –lope, a Kansas euphemism for bagging one's grinder, a.k.a. priming the piston, a.k.a. surf & turf, a.k.a. yoking the oxen, a.k.a. loping the mule

& one of its legs would rest on a rusty axle timed to fracture exactly x-days after your y-year warranty

elapsed to guarantee more production of 100% natural &
organic American steel livestock

exposed corrosion, we based
blueprints on a day laborer

placing ball bearings at odd angles
[a laugh like Butthead's] huh huh [echoes
Beavis] he said, "balls"

every grindstone cowboy needs one
plaid snap shirt w/ every purchased pentalope
             fourteen *eat me* installments—this beast
                 "of humor dry & blackest bile"

I once fed a chicken a dinosaur's leg

true story: & for a lifetime
compliance we'll throw in this wristwatch

                        all work is on the hour

this here is certified pentalope, all pure USA RDA because our production facility only believes in Kansas blue-grain, grass-less fed.

*

Acknowledgements

Part of this book first appeared in an elderly man's underwear.

Raved a Colorado bar girl, after buying Larry a beer: "I swear part of this book so déjà vued me, I thought I was smelling the inside of an oyster vessel."

Which could have been a shell, out of whose clam-clamps some of these poems escaped.

Your thoughts, initially.

Some of this I originally wrote on obscure anti-capitalist pamphlets variously distributed around Seattle coffee houses & menus describing American microbrews, particularly mouthfeel.

Thank you in particular to Ideology™: Brewing Consent & Conformity for the Post-Person Age.

As you might recall, I used pop-theory phrases always italicized or directly quoted to get you into bed.

*

A few weeks ago, while we were having drinks, the editor of a small, online literary journal confessed, "it's been years since I've been floored by a book of contemporary poetry." She continued, "we publish these writers, one to five poems, & I get excited about their work. But then when I see a whole collection, I'm mostly disappointed." We went on to discuss poets—many by name; many that you read/will read, many published by prominent independent and collegiate poetry presses, whose work excites but inevitably bores, not unlike the $10 cocktails we were knocking back.

That night, I realized my own reading experience aligns with the editor's & so many of my other writer friends; contemporary poetry, especially the "full-length" collection, often leaves me blue-balled (SIDE NOTE—I should confess most novels do this, too; if DeLillo scrapped half of *Underworld* or Murakami *1Q84*, those novels night deserve the acclaim they received; however, every word of McCarthy's *Blood Meridian* is indispensable, *The Waves, The Waves*). Blaming pop culture or technological impacts on attention span shifts the responsibility onto the reader & may ultimately facilitate the continued mediocrity of 21st Century verse. I'm convinced the reason that so many books feel like orgasms never achieved is in the division between multiple aesthetics erroneously conceived as being mutually exclusive.

I've come to view contemporary poetry as falling into two camps, which I term the neo-conservative (sometimes neo-traditional) & avant-garde. To channel Reginald Shepherd's brilliant essay "On Difficulty in Poetry," what I really should have labeled the camps were capitalist poetics & elitist poetics. While I tend toward the intellectual, erudite avant-garde for my personal reading, I can't abandon the notion that most of this poetry feels vapid, unemotional, and disconnected from the reality of the larger human forces it seeks to engage. At its worst, elitist poetic ideologies claim to champion social movements to eradicate marginalization but are themselves so removed that they don't understand how the individual experiencing oppression views the day-to-day struggle. Human rights become reduced to a mind-game, & when feeling is extracted, any change—even if it reverses the abuses of a previous power group—will dehumanize even as it claims to promote the greater good. Shepherd referred to this type of poetry as "obscure," which he calls "a fault."

It's all too easy to view capitalist poetics as unsatisfying. By capitalist poetics, I mean the poetry that opens itself up to the experiences of all, which is often an Everyman, still whiter & with greater penis envy than ever. This is the poetry that one reads once & immediately understands. The writer-grandfather takes the reader by the hand, uses sensory images to explain the scene for several, equally paced lines, & delivers an epiphany as the poem comes to a close. The body poetic leaves the "grandchild's" worldview forever changed just as it affirms the "grandfather's" conservative vision. That such poetry tends toward melodrama (i.e. "grandmother's" life might just be symbolized by the chipped rim of that exquisite blue tea cup) is a risk of this poetry of pathos, one often realized. Like its economic counterpart, capitalist poetics ostensibly champions the causes of everyone, yet in "dumbing down," it ends up espousing only the beliefs of a guiding power group, marginalizing as the stanzas unfold.

I agree with Shepherd that difficulty "is an essential feature of poetry." Rather than taking sides in this debate—Susan Howe is too obscure; Billy Collins is too easy—we need to look at what both aesthetics offer. Although prone to sentimentalizing, capitalist poetics are imbued with evoking emotional responses; their poetry has its nexus in the heart. Although prone to pomposity, elitist poetics move by engaging the mind; their poetry drives the brain's neural firings. A synthesis of the two is what much contemporary poetry seems to lack. As a result, we quickly forget poems or feel reduced to aborted fetuses floating in jars of words (SIDENOTE—I once described attending an elitist poetry reading as being like that image given its predilection toward monotony over performance). Either way, we are isolated from the concerns of <u>all</u>.

To create an arresting full-length book, poets should create a "difficult" poetry that makes itself emotionally available without opacity or perpetuating the Everyman myth. The individual poem should feature openings for readers to enter & play in the poem's space, never bounded by linear time or history, or the extremities of reason or emotion. As a whole, the arranged, individual poems offer a poetry that is connected to people without dumbing itself down to promote a guiding power structure. When thinking about recent books, three of the more prominent to achieve the above are Maggie Nelson's *Bluets*, Christina Davis's *An Ethic*, & Claudia Rankine's *Citizen*. Many others (published by small &/or independent presses) have also achieved such synthesis, works of true "difficulty" that make their gifts thought & felt & reaffirm poetry's humanizing presence in an increasingly stratified mechanical world.

*

Night Moves (for William Carlos Williams)

Reading the modernists,
I began suspecting I was
stable, desiring
your sleeping body, looking

across wet fields at chickens
hung for feathering

& discovering completeness
in my mirror slightly

fogged from a morning shower,
your snores lifting
off the couch where we made
our genitals evaporate

near the slender lawn, glisten
our glazed surrender

to our selected fetishes
that will never define us

that we left wanting
fractured our red wagon's hold.

*

Easy, Rider

We begin by discussing in Kansas
oil fields that will power the collapsible
horse-gone-electric, each wire

a caste to implement as we lay track
west, mesas never acceptable
as limit. The native labor's grown too smart
we'll import workers who don't know

they're slaves; these rocks suffice for wages;
this postcard of our suburban dwellings
to which they'll aspire. We control outflow

of babies & wives—husbands to keep
some sense of autonomy, but no one in control;
anatomical knowledge undermines the gendered
echo of authority. Every four years

we will stage a great robbery
but with natives confined
to fistfight over rations, the enemy

is actually ourselves, though disguised
as alien. Check your six-shooters;
actual violence is no longer necessary. We'll invent

controls over our bodies to dictate a dialectical
distraction as we investigate the theft
choices only ever illusioned

that they might have while the mechanical equine
chugs on, only true border is the saddle we sit on.
*

Here's another scenario: there isn't an overpass bridge in sight. I'm climbing the keyhole route of Long's Peak, following the bull's eyes painted on rocks rubbed bald by others before me. The exposure past the Agnes Vaille Hut features 1,000' drops & sheer, vertical cliffs above alpine lakes & scree fields below. The trail through sections like the Narrows is roughly the size of an average city sidewalk. The ascent is challenging enough, but in addition to my backpack, I carry the fear that I'll jump.

According to a study conducted by Florida State University's psychology department, my impulse to leap is caused by my misinterpretation of the instinctual safety signal, that I feel fear not because I am tempted but because I thought I was tempted. Counter-theories suggest that I process jumping for the thrill, much like going to an amusement park, or that some sort of cognitive dissonance exists between my instincts saying "jump back" & my remaining on the ledge, which I momentarily read as a compulsion to "jump forward."
None of these academic approaches feel satisfactory to rationalize my desire to throw myself over.

Sometimes, I lucid dream. When I do, one of the activities I indulge in is bounding. I propel myself upward as if in flight, but rather than remaining suspended, I float back to the ground. As I touch down, I project myself up again, a trampoline-like effect. The dream sensation I experience keeps me returning.

An airiness, a lightness comes over my body, and replicating this is what causes me to look down now at Blue Lake, to imagine hovering above the peak itself, arching down toward Hallet or Flattop or another peak below, touching down lightly on the balls of my feet to

spring up again as if I can choose when I come down. If
I do.

*

The Lettered Hollow

The recurrence of yourself appears
as an architecture of masks. I'm guilty

assuming order in facial structures
how another mimics your lips
placed over your lips to preclude

avowal. Once, we traveled west
to deconstruct a prose
about a traveler who knew post-persons
by their bone structure

which was always
a slip of the tongue. We studied
several formal nudes. I thought language

belonged to the body, a paragraph

I'm forever trying to write

but to look is to boundary.
We bordered on terror, our birthday
suits insubstantial for shelter
how this nude stands to face wind
reminds me of you. Exposure

our only fear, name
walled in our throats' confessions.

*

A Poststructuralist Study of Fantasy Novel Archetypes

the frail, deranged mage who enacts his deviant fetishes
    on the leather wounds of children;

the virtuous paladin who flogs herself to sleep while
    listening to squirt-inducing anal orgasms;

the elf, a victim of oppressive factory labor & later the
    justification for skin-whitening cream, both

misconstrued by heads-of-state to declare war on fat men in red suits;

the noble savage, of which so many popular landscapes are named;

the evil of dubious origin, typically wielding advanced technology that exploits the popular landscapes, leading to the appropriation of tear-shedding "savagery" by the heads-of-state who will, in turn, relegate "savagery" to plastic bubble environments to better place flags;

the race of little people, who always get their pubic beards plucked out in the end.

*

THE YELLOW DANCE (FOR AARON APPS)

Is, I believe, a grey action
feeding you on this rain/hail/rail
camping trip

                    (do you know that bluejeans
                fail to offer the most crotch-stretch

I remember a poem about how those titties
buff my hubcaps
                            (& do you know
                beershits become poems but ↔

desired this roommate of yours (I had
a girlfriend & walking home

our first Colorado snow) her name

might have been someone I'd wed—I wish
I could have shown you

                            (streets much too cement
                these cracks & I swear by walking

actual trees

to hear you read your garden
you'd look miserable by that tent

now an argument for leaving
me who under other tutelage ∴ this

                             *

"The vivid rhetoric of terror was a first step in the slow process toward American Democracy."—Susan Howe, *My Emily Dickinson*

"To exist, humanely, is to name the world, to change it. Once named, the world in its turn reappears to the namers as a problem & requires of them a new naming."—Paolo Freire, *Pedagogy of the Oppressed*

"Dialogue is the encounter between men, mediated by the world, in order to rename the world."—Ibid.

The Political Dimension of Poetry I: Poetry enables the writer & reader to establish a dialogue "mediated by the world in order to name the world" (Paolo Freire). An elitist poetics obscures its dialogue from the reader, preventing the reader from participating in the naming. What passes for avant-garde is a solitary naming, a verbal exercise on the part of the writer signifying (achieving?) nothing. A capitalist poetics forces its dialogue onto the reader, conforming the reading to its naming pattern. What passes for neo-traditional is an imposed naming, an action that renders the reader object.

Ethics in Poetry: the dialogue is a participatory language act whereby the writer & reader establish & re-establish mutually agreed on patterns, processes.

Ambiguity in Poetry: an invitation to the reader into the poem's body—which is never a limit—where dialogic naming appears & instantly requires a new naming. Elitist & capitalist languages end the dialectic.

Negation in Poetry: the refusal to name can facilitate dialogue only so long as it calls attention to the language informing the dialogue. Poetry exists in language but must never be thought stable. Where dialogue does not occur, negation may be used to liberate the *reader-turned-object*.

A Grounded Abstraction: the dialogue exists in the eternal now associated with animal history. Its subject may present historical or future, but the writer-reader dialogue always occurs in the present. Language's slipperiness must recreate the present. If it does not, there is no dialogue & is instead a verbalism that will hook itself to then or soon. This fixes the terms of the dialogue to past modes of naming, chiefly those established by academies (elitism) or a power majority (capitalism), or allows for coercive naming, which constitutes discourse (domination, debate, & authority).

A Poem's Difficulty: is allowing the <u>world</u> to mediate the dialogue, to the writer & reader coming to the poem-space with attentive presence & without threat of swinging the power dynamic to favor one over the other, to make both equal participants in the naming.

The Political Dimension of Poetry II: Must always necessitate a revolutionary act conducted in the ever-present dialogue in the irreducible names of love & justice.

*

A Minor's Archeology Always Involves Cracking Whips

My gun went off because I called in a sick day

        1st excavation: deciphering your arch's
        petroglyphs that haven't been carved out

        I'm talking your irrelevant spine
        red line that grids our world

Southwestern Utah, I can't believe parents march their children toward this fallen, angled landing. The US government outsourced all relics herein discovered to generic wood panel

who controls the grid, controls the names

        2nd excavation: I don't bake
        my own pound cake

        slicing strawberries inside
        chilled Darwin

squealed funky feces-flinging, root my monkey

Daddy's home to call you by an arbitrary state name

you'll forever reclaim your 3rd:

I wanted to be a paleontologist
whose ice cream instigated

T-Rex sparring until we became a common
spare-rib scavenger.

*

ANIMAL HISTORIES

To say the moon might be alien
visible only when cut through pine

in Pacific NW forests
race of night-people seen
most light. They are always light

their terrestrial history
of catch & release narrated by earthmen
disguised as conversions, their world-
god of was & will be. A woman
reported cyclic attraction
to moon's appearing above tree-line,
which her husband censured
as heresy. Indigenous hearsay
suggests she met lunatics
who claimed treaties read the same

wooded paths spoke differently
dawn till dusk. This woman outlived dirt

claimed sky-beings illuminated
her nether places, restored her
to sinew, bone. When her husband died

he became an architecture. Many
occupying him discovered her story
as proof to manifest clear-

cutting so their prayers expanded

electrical grids. Through windows
notched in his spine they fired
scattershot at moon
always missing but in time convinced
themselves their perforations were not
foreign. The occupiers' record
claims she both begins & ends

though in truth her elastic tongue
is always turning on itself
projecting what they term hysteria.

V

Mule Dream

Came on a midnight clearing
grass so sharp it slit lips, defied
making cud. Flies attack

scar tissue & to whip the brand
only leaves tail hair
caught in contours

this field where every pasture's
gone to fence. There's a limit
to when & how much

we drink. I know by now the cattle's
disappearances equal no returns
horses I'm certain

have a hoof in it. The oil rubs help
prevent new bites but sting
open wounds, singe

them closed in summer. This afternoon
sizzles the farmhouse window
kids who curse me, call me

rocks thrown & blades
caught in my teeth
I keep my mouth shut. Weeds

surround my wheel-less cart
wait out my days this morning
still wet with this evening's snow.

*

Dedication

To Hamlin's children, those seduced souls sealed behind a rock, doomed to sleep in shadows while the goat-footed piper taps alien rhythms from imagined hills.

*

Mostly we talked about digressions, the pen for hand & thumb for a fool. Like how the word PULP appeared etched into the porcelain near the flusher's silver base. I stared at it while I peed, thinking about the dream I'd had of an alternate 1960s. Two teens from Kansas arrived in New York to live with a chef & a poet. The poet made language projects resembling postcards, music by negating the expectation of sound. His lover, the chef, often made fun of him for always using words as other than to mean. I took the toilet engraving as proving this project's existence. After all, I had selected it randomly, one of several in Denver International Airport. I told you about it; you texted, "heh. sounds like time to get back to work."

*

CIVIL WAR Z

At the Oasis of the Plains
we met John Brown. He told us

his plan for a New Kansas
although we weren't sure if he spoke

through his mouth or neck-
scar. We wore the same Carhartt's.

"My family's soil's been hell
on preserving my knees,"

spoke his lips or his jugular,
"have you ever seen gangrene?"

Once he came back as Bobby Kennedy,
his chest had more bullet holes

than we could count & each
shred of skin a Bible verse. Frankly

we were grossed out. The line at Starbucks
inched forward, he spurted

pus as he ordered, singing
"If I only had the President's brain."
*

"The only people in this country who are asked to be non-violent are black people."—Malcom X

An absolving activism is precipitated by fear of the other, is wearing t-shirts in selfies proclaiming with hands raised (in unnecessary defense), is an aqueous solidarity, for the language employed by such activists only reinforces proof that America needs sensationalism to preserve systemic othering. Every few years a riot. Every few years a voicing.

The outrage expressed reduced to Twitter; in 160 characters or less the American police state. Bored white kids becoming another preamble; things white people like, a beating so offensive that to oppose it unburdens white guilt.

When Fred Phelps, Sr. of the Westboro Baptist Church was gaining notoriety, my father argued that Phelps's message of extreme hate actually excused the beliefs of closet homophobes. They could condemn public messages that gays deserved hell, but they could still feel internal, unvoiced discomfort at a same-sex couple holding hands in the park.

Trump may produce an equal effect. Differentiate yourself from the open racist by condemning this one act while being complicit in how many more. There's a black kid who didn't die of 17 blows to his head named anonymous & we'll let it slide.

Once the presses cease coverage, will white America go back to its hip hop & sports? Will white America talk about its black or brown friend & secretly desire a white quarterback or point guard because "they know better how to run the show?" And if they don't there's a white coach or an electorate who'll find a suitable replacement.

You may or may not hear the ousted player's name again.

*

"We're Going to Need Another Timmy"

Cavemen clubbed the last dinosaur
to rubble, made foot-

operated cars & erected

stone tablets to dictate the mastodons'

language. Reduced
to ordinary elephants

they could be collared, encouraged
in their pursuits of painting

& sculpture—arts cavemen
pillaged. Sympathizng

with the mastodons' plight
was popular among Neolithic youth

so annually elders charged
a calf with resisting arrest,

an offense punishable by public
spearing. The youth expressed outrage

went back to literally
crunching numbers, discussing

sabertooth cats, fucking
themselves to sleep.

*

SLAVE STATE (ODE TO FOX NEWS)

Anomalous protrusion, a skeletal
army discovered *in apparati*
a locking mechanism, decision

of whom to shoot & where. A choke collar
sometimes placebo
controlling *en masse* the receiver
from trampling the pylon. His

outstretched arm, his delinquency
contributes to concussion.

We cheer the stretcher bearing him.
The crew, their forearms

theatrical white—this stadium

the flyover a Whitman
blind to America whose bone soldiers
democratize our cheers, our decibels
concussed in the barrel

anticipating the next flag thrown.

*

"I, John Brown, am now quite *certain* that the crimes of this *guilty land* will never be purged away but w/ blood. I had, as I now think vainly, flattered myself that without very much bloodshed it might be done."
—John Brown, *Life & Letters*

America provides evidence of action so appalling everyone rages. Another black man dies on YouTube. Another Muslim can't re-enter. Another Mexican child is separated from her parents. We go back to leaving Margarita a list of weekly chores in our Telluride ski home, unoccupied all but one month a year.

Power structures in the US bank on rage's diminishing return. Power will overstep its bounds to kill an innocent for its own preservation. Attention to extremes diverts attention from the day-to-day micro-aggressions. The day-to-day becomes codified—is extreme in its non-extremism. Is acceptable insofar as "it could be worse."

Outrage on behalf of the other will reduce to "at least nobody's getting killed."

Martyrs are created from the images of those who actually died for a purpose for which all would die, symbolically, to preserve those who, literally, didn't die but to justify their privilege.

*

The Hype of a New World, One We Can Both Assemble

I am blessing, king, vast desert
eaten—a body primed

to plug the sacrilege—a climbing
rope in belay device too small

portray myself as ass crack.
Wilderness, very

everyman a saint, compulsory
falling, breakage at the heels.

*

I fear Trump's Presidency, the very narrative of it; which is to say we must resist the historicizing of the act into part of the National story because history is outside of the present & therefore always reinforces the ideology of the power group. A riot or march is rooted in beginning & end; a revolution follows the cycle of breath. By attending to each inhale & exhale the mind, as both forward & backward reasoning organ, aligns with the body, an instinctive sack whose appetite is the current sensation. A revolution does not have an instigating act or a future agenda; the revolution inspires/respires & its focus to its own presence determines the degree of its success, its revolutionary nature. Compassion, its only cause; in drawing awareness to our breath we acknowledge others' breathing & the plot elements of race, gender, ethnicity, class, etc. fall away until we recognize the rights of all to live outside of designations, time, & story. The poem's dialogic, lingual space affords mutual breath—the writer & reader sharing the same inhalation/exhalation apparatus—at once in the throat & out of the throat; thus, the poem is always a revolutionary act. The Political Dimension of Poetry III.

*

Family Sitcom

In matrimony light we begin
to let our bodies grow
out of our nakedness

puzzle whose pieces
no longer interlock, a fish

dead in night-
stand bowl. If we get fat,
we get funny; if we
get kids, we can moralize

driving the sedan
through the garage door is okay,
baking your brother into a brioche
is okay. Here's our picture
in front of "Welcome to the State"
that proves it so. Remember

when I got dark, asked you to erase
my cartoon dad, lager cans

all drinking the same. I was raised
by my two uncles who for laughs
had careers in comedy & modeling

it's a wonder I roll over
reach for you, a dog
secretly desiring the last time

we wore pajamas.

*

SLAVE STATE 2.0 (ODE TO CNN)

In the otherwise reality
where we're all superheroes
my power is ambiguously inflecting my voice
so as to cause the listener to shit
& cum simultaneously
providing me with 15 seconds of disgusted ecstasy
to subdue them, which is why I think
people used to tell me I belong
on radio. Jesus Christ

anticipated Houdini & came back
as David Blaine. Everyone's searching
for a gilled breathing apparatus—
Blaine swears he can recap the poles
but as backup we need actual mutations
to believe poetry
might resurrect us & launder
our stained underwear into the sweet
sepulchered hereafter.

*

When art is propaganda, the poem must recognize not only its political but ethical dimensions. The poem brings forth speech out of blank space; it is a denial of silence & in its linguistic turns a refutation (or calling attention to) of language's staleness. As readers, we allow the poem to enter our throats & dwell, bonding us with the poet & the source of the poetic gift. In this united, eternal presence, language (which can be verbal or non-verbal) is at constant play until we are dropped again into the silence, now a meditative space, alone to contemplate. In this sense, silence serves to give thoughtful rest.

But silence can also be used to cut off, isolate, restrict, repress—as can acts of language if they become too codified. Just as we need poetry's voice to cut through the silence of those who believe they aren't racist or perpetuate racism through inaction or ignorance, we need poetry's critics to feel empowered to express their objections.

The poem's political & ethical force is felt most fully when its form & content destabilize through a worded incision on the page, achieving in the writer & reader recognitions of presence & oneness, before their solitary return to the emptiness of the margins, the place demanding a new, mediated, dialogic renaming. This is the genius of poetry.

*

CHOKEHOLD 2.0

In the beta version, you can customize
your favorite Judiciary Institutional
Systems Maintainer (JISM) on his quest
to crush the apparatuses
various extraterrestrials use
to breathe. With updated features:

—no differentiation between innocent & guilty; squeeze first & ask questions later
—watch your victims' air supplies dwindle as you bear down
—brag about your kills on social media
—new, harder to identify crimes; don't worry, choke them all!
—dozens of new moves based on hours of watching actual law enforcement footage

—adjustable difficulty including "alien profiling mode"
—now multiplayer; choke within your own geographic boundaries or all over the world!

You won't play a more realistic game this year!
Feel your electronic control
device shake as your JISM
delivers the fatal blow. Watch
as your JISM asphyxiates
without fear of legal recourse!
Anyone in your way will literally choke
thanks to your JISM.

Protect the planet while you make the planet
desire protection from you. Deploy
your JISM everywhere.

(Best experienced on American National User Systems platforms).

*

Children of the Revolution

"Capital burns off the nuance in a culture"—Don
DeLillo, *Underworld*

When a gendered economy becomes
the new capital
sex is always political. This, the premise

of the indie film
we'll see after eating vegan
approximations of flesh

tofu has only one porous
genital. In the theater lobby
we're surrounded
by photographs of old people
whose work defined their relations
all with such rough hands.
Popcorn prices fluctuate,

digitized beginning of sneak
dietetics, we've barely

sat down before we forget the hunter

emerging with quarry. As a child
I had to differentiate
grandma from grandpa as other
than skin.

*

When an established Northern Colorado, mission-style burrito chain decided to expand into Fort Collins, a group of citizens protested that its name, Illegal Pete's, was culturally insensitive to Mexicans and Mexican-Americans. Never mind that the business had operated for several years in Denver & Boulder without incident. Never mind that Pete is the name of the owner's father & the "Illegal" comes from a bar in a Hunter S. Thompson book. Never mind that the cuisine is more reminiscent of San Francisco than anywhere South of the Border. In the age of sensitivity, argued the protestors, the name simply isn't acceptable.

Leading the protest, or at least one of its most vocal supporters, is a tenure-track professor in the Rhetoric & Composition branch of Colorado State University's

English department. As an academic, he presents a compelling case for the name change, full of big words & erudite theory; however, like many arguments developed behind collegiate walls, his position lacks examples of real world impact.

Granted: "illegal" is a term used as an offensive, derogatory metonymy toward Latinos, many of them legal residents & many more who have been in the US for several generations.

Granted: for the reasons listed above (see para. 1), the business isn't guilty of intentional racism.

Granted: intent seldom matters (rightfully so) in discussing micro-aggressions.

Honestly, I'm neither convinced or unconvinced that Illegal Pete's needs to change its name. The academic is right to voice his concerns just as Pete Turner is justified in elucidating his reasons to keep his business's name as is. To me, these protests are just another example of academics being disconnected from the concerns that actually matter to & impact real people.

Granted: Paolo Freire describes intellectuals as "well-intentioned but not infrequently alienated from the reality of the people."

Granted: Claudia Rankine's book *Citizen* makes partially transparent an exigent conversation about race, yet some of its scholarly argot may render it unheard outside of lecture halls.

Granted: Leroy Gomez, a Fort Collins resident, points out that "thousands of Mexican migrants in Northern Colorado who work on farms are seen as a regrettable necessity & often treated as such." Gomez goes on to identify where academics should place attention, on the real-world issues that oppress tremendous numbers of individuals but white-washed America ignores.

Bickering about a name is what enables power structures to continue to oppress; the perceived racism (if even there) may be altered, but the actual racism remains untouched because so much energy is expended fighting a trivial battle. As a writer, I do believe in the power of words to shape reality (though the question of words giving rise to reality or reality giving rise to words is enormously difficult to navigate); however, changing the name of a restaurant isn't going to impact how Fort Collins residents view the oppressed in their community. Nor is a name change going to affect how the oppressed view themselves in relation to their oppressors.

The insidious nature of oppression is its ability to divert resources & human compassion from issues that have higher stakes; for example, how without exploitative agricultural practices a lot of white people would feel incredibly inconvenienced at the grocery store.

*

FARM TO FUCK

Course I
Poached Quail Egg served over Warm Greens pulled from your wallet

Large bills only, please.

Course II
*Puree of Roasted Cauliflower accompanied by Croquettes d*Privilège

Artisanal potatoes: so succulent & rich.

Course III
Local Pan-Seared Trout w/ Toasted Almonds

We own the water rights to what was your favorite fishing hole.

Course IV
Asian-Spiced Roast w/ Cilantro Chimichurri
& Broiled Asparagus (just so we haven't appropriated this entire dish)

Course V
Rib of some little pest we killed because it was wreaking havoc at the farm, chewing up our $5 leaves of lettuce, so now here it is w/ some KC-Style BBQ sauce because we want to look like we're in touch w/ our potential blue collar patrons

Best enjoyed w/ a 12 oz. Pabst ($7.00)

Course VI
Strawberry-Fluffed Air

Thank you for spending a week's wages at our restaurant. Since we know you'll leave empty, we invite you to visit our sister venture, Big Angus, an all-GMO burger and fry joint in the newly gentrified W.E.B. Dubois district.

*

BLINK

All art proposes violence
an imagined thicket
growing over real brambles
that actually barb, goat-
heads over-twining the wood. Forest

replaced as is, undergrowth
substituting under-

growth, kudzu where we pictured
a new Florida, swamps

stand-ins for fountains & we age
according to each material

synapse firing
across blank space to know

the garden is
as we left it
erased in its own emergence
a shade between every summer
sprouted, wilted, wintering.

*

LASCAUX 2.0

We sat along the old road
humming what we could remember
of birds, when trees still bore
names. You had an antique

whiteness to your teeth, blue
veins that camouflaged
your arms. We'd never crossed
over to pasture, but air

was warm, soil
rich, & in caves not far

horses that'd gallop across fields
when drawn.

*

self-awareness through solitary contemplation
    → the modern condition
self-awareness through relational properties
    → the postmodern condition
self-awareness through recognition of post-personhood
    → the post-person condition

*

Larry Lazarus texted his friend: Do you ever experience while reading, this strange perceptiveness about how weird it is to read, how odd to make sense of an arrangement—angles & curves organized into patterns of varying lengths, those patterns further sequenced into lines & lastly chunks that while isolated flow into one another, archipelagos of geometric scrawl that at a glance & under scrutiny are without sense? Do you ever think about how bizarre reading is that you are so hyper aware of the action that your mind actually starts to disconnect from those angles & curves & you feel like at any moment you might forget the very behavior of reading & just stare at the scrawl like an idiot failing to recognize that his shadow emanates from him & is not something separate, full of meaning?

*

Book for No One (from *Post-Person Linguistics*)

I was born inside a stereo. Thumps
reverberated my spine, low
deep bass throbbing my temples, how good
you look in your Sunday gown belting

admonishments to an unseen hand
the knobs. Frequencies
a frequent crackle distorted by sudden talk
when the needle tickles the old soul
station out of South Mobile. Driving
twang to Telluride, true strings
strung along the Appalachians'
teeth, your hands beating rhythm
how sweet your tongue just behind.
A devil waits where chords
cross the way he'll save you selling
treble to thrum your bones. My ears
pop between fluid, how lovely your voice
echoes off plywood & when I sing I swear
my breath is fire, my feet
tap until dark dies, morning.

*

FROM *THE MECHANICAL RECORDS*

I spent some years outside the glass
wiring my own jaw shut

alone to my primordial miscalculations
I saw fingers for what they are

      (how voluptuous the lazy bride & all her white
              hours her groomed grasps

we all wanted to grow
into Our Fathers are
hollows the stillborn photograph

         fishermen believe, still, that quietude
         overflows their nets w/ maimed disciples

a tourniquet,   a stitching, a pelvis
torqueing the bridegroom's genocide

      this he calls love

          (I said to my father, water
      ceded a plant & that material spring
        accompanies a babbling, a damage

we are a reliquary of who & how we love

        today I am stressing
        an alphabet in order
        to summon a lover

        w/ plaits made for whipping
        w/ shoulders made for breaking
        w/ a torso bendable

as conch   (as ear

please deliver me news of today's patricide
flower girls have cast their shell hooks
into sea my mouth
is isthmus   the sound

(some waves lapped then at the shore & I told my father that I had grown tired of shade, but I don't think he heard. He kept looking at his palms like he mangled me. His fingers smelled cloven, like something green.

VI

NOTE FROM LARRY LAZARUS:

These poems are not substitutes for action. They are not intended to absolve you from keeping your yoga class in child's pose while outside the studio a ragman shits on the wet sidewalk. Nor do they excuse you from referring to Victoria as Victor because you thought she was a he by her collared button-ups & loose-crotched Levis in the treble that answered your questions unwaveringly. This work does not absolve you from experiencing privilege & when you talk about privilege, social justice, Marxism with your community college students—mostly international students or students of color—you are not exempted from owning "white savior."

Writing *PULP* does not make of your house an awning, does not darken your skin. Save that role for what masquerades as art, for meta-justices that enable ideological enslavement that translates to exploitation, oppression, & injustice.

The problem is not the police but the state they serve.

So long as poetry becomes a hipster's lament, three masked men with shotguns will continue to raid the basement apartment across the street in broad daylight, authorities will keep killing black kids who wave knock-off Super Soakers, the yoga studio walls will exclude any who can't afford the $25 per one-hour class session because the belly hungers. The heart yearns. From the mouths of those who control, words are regurgitated as imaginary bread.

*

THIS POEM IS ABOUT POETRY (FOR THE VOICE OF MY GENERATION)

To declare you are dead necessitates a language
for infant birthed in autobiographical fiction
by which I mean subtext

by which I've been doing acts
of alphabetting. I've seen this name
bleached across mirrors, fog

reads 10:04 the afternoon before a tornado

wrecked a barn I witnessed
splinters become a twinkling gulf

my son you have already propagated. My girl
you are an ear through which squeals
write themselves into another art
party—I'm pretty sure I drank all the Tecate here.

Clad me in cutoffs, where you so easily quoted
Snoop Doggy Dogg, this literature
is begging for color, a dinosaur
within the imagination of an actual child

who might have had flesh & someday crawled
this shrinking ocean reeking of unreconstructed shores.

*

"I'm Your Huckleberry"
                    —Val Kilmer (as Doc Holliday)

Let's duel over who can hold doors
ajar for the most women,

old ones as well as hotties
because let's be honest we're both looking for

where beauty intersects drunkeness
so we can unholster

pneumatic respirators, too long
in dry climates among gold-

hearted hookers. I mean, let's stand
each other down, this 4-

way intersection oblivious
to horns. Won't I

do some fancy revolver tricks
with a cocktail napkin, sentimental

after discovering we're Eskimo brothers
who for linguistic exercise rape

each other humorously over our fantasy
football teams' actual production.

*

Plain, Unassorted White Citizen (for Ed Dorn)

Always takes you to Pho Than's
where he can order by number
the waiters, he says, have short-term memories.

He takes all his first dates here
& anyway every white girl
is a white girl
even the Vietnamese woman

he dated while teaching English
which he tells you, "this crap
ain't even close to authentic"
but he likes it because it reminds him of the other

life. You don't have any say in hearing
cross-country backpacking trips
"they prefer that you don't talk like them,"

he tells you about a poem
narrating "the difference

is they add more herbs in Saigon."
You find this interesting & let him
show you how to garnish

just as later he'll order
your cocktail at the fern bar
trying hard not to be a fern bar & you'll nod

inside another story knowing
he owns a record player
plasma TV, has fine oak bookshelves

memorized three songs on guitar
"to seal the deal" lying on his bed
in underwear his mother
gave him last Christmas.

*

Here's another scenario: On a chilly, early-January morning, I'm biking through Seattle's U District. I teach a 6:00 am yoga class twice a week &, unless I've woken up late or it's dumping rain, I leave my car at home. Though the studio is about a mile away, I don't walk. Even when school is in session, the sidewalks & streets are mostly empty at this hour. The people up & about aren't taking well-groomed dogs out before work or running off the weight accrued over their indulgent holidays.

I pull my bike to a stop at a new traffic light installed at the corner of 12th Ave NE & 50th. Before the city altered the intersection, I could bring my bike to a slow coast (feet still on the pedals), a pause long enough to look both ways prior to pedaling through. Now, the timer-operated light is generally red for north-south traffic, necessitating a full stop. Although there's a YMCA on the corner that opens early for workouts, I prefer not to idle here.

A string of armed robberies—a frequent event in this neighborhood where college students, with their tablets & smartphones, make excellent theft targets—have been lighting up UW's text alert system on my then-partner's phone. The victims have been alone, on foot, knocked out or threatened with weapons from twilight until dawn.

"You should be okay on bike," my downstairs neighbor assures me. But if I stop for a light, can I ride away in time?

Near the button to activate a pedestrian crossing & accelerate the light's timer, a man mumbles to himself. I can barely see his lips move under his scraggly facial hair. He keeps his hands deep in the pockets of his oversized coat. This makes sense given the temperature, but he appears to be rummaging for something. He looks at me.

More to say something than to acknowledge, I greet him, ask how he's doing.
He says, "Cold. How are you?"

"Tired," I answer, though my knuckles remain white on the handlebars, my right foot tense on the pavement, poised to push off.

"Hey," he says, fingers still fishing & fidgeting out of my view, "Happy New Year."

The light turns green. "You too," I reply before riding off, my heart thumping with a sensation like wanting to receive an unexpected, friendly text from a once-familiar friend. Or grabbing the obese, mentally-disabled kid's balls because if you can take him down without flinching, you've made it to your elementary school's in-crowd.

*

The Last Peasant

Was a spectacle on Astroturf
made of wax
milking near the placard
that historicized his origins
in plastic grains, sun
painted between horizon

to complete the diorama. In this museum
each patron wears a suit
always reminded

of walls while eating snacks

produced in absence
of seasoning. Audio streams
reduce the last peasant
to narration. He begins & ends
daily the ancient world
where hands were material,

not collected capital. His relics
are representations. The consumers
cannot imagine using them, converse
in traditional tongues

identity's extent, artificial
now as to then.

*

The Political Dimension of Poetry IV: writing the perfect poem is impossible because to do so would obliterate distinction, would pull separateness—including the poet's own self-consciousness—into a consummated, erotically violent annihilation. Such a poem would, in fact, end the world. What is then required of the poet in order to make of the poem a merging, a word that linguistically & spatially becomes world? A willing sacrifice of self-consciousness as in the moment of erotic crisis, where to pleasure the other we fully become the other. Self-consciousness is understood, then, as a tangible illusion, & though a body exits another body (as reader from writer, poet from poem) a recognition of unity, of sameness.

Through this sameness we understand suffering & joy as universal, so must act always to alleviate the former to promote the latter. The Ethical Dimension of Poetry.

*

Residence Evil (for John Berger)

Taken together, living smells—
rainwater, feces, & the decaying
rat in the bathroom—lack of
residency; occupying space
as dwellers do, asleep
on cardboard. Light

does not illuminate moving
dust like in homes
they construct to name aromas
in burn scars
grandma's splotched hands.

New high-rises have odorless walls
concrete barricades w/ sensors
that can detect the silence
of too much static, transmit
to opaque monitors eyes

of those who cannot conform
the contained. Poem is
pupil, dwellers
recite them in glances
sometimes in plain view. The gentrified

have no literature
all their walls project
without presence, nothingness
a material gaze.

*

To believe a ranch kid from Kansas would grow up to write poems. I would like to be encased in what those hills, surrounding us on all sides, meant as covered in wildflowers or hoarfrost they held time. The Pied Piper taught me the song's value, purifying & sinister. There's always a you.

Age five, I won a coloring contest to impress my mother's intern. I stayed within the lines. I used colors that represented what the Easter Bunny actually looked like. Among my competition's Technicolor scribbles, my poster looked stripped from a museum. An experiment in realism—I read my heartland audience well & I won. My mother's intern gave me a kiss on the cheek, but she still wouldn't marry me. She still returned to Las Vegas. Leaving me with a stuffed dog, its arms Velcroed around its oddly humanoid puppy.

Maybe that's when I started to abandon the real. Maybe that began my attraction to poems. You can ask me—as the 25th issue of *Free Verse* posed to Larry— "what is the work of poetry?" & I'll tell you the Pied Piper opened a hole in limestone & children followed him there. Of course, they were scared. Their lure had no face, a body that lurched as though sewn full of music. A thread dangled but not one dared unravel it, so raptured & terrified they wet themselves wide-eyed & looking. Even as the cave closed behind them, at the shadows painting familiar images on rock. In the darkness, they could no longer separate themselves from each other or from the piping grown frenzied, arrhythmic.

They clutched each other & knew they filled the entire space. They listened until they could see themselves in the song, lifting upward, outward, through cracks in earth, into sky where they dissolved.

*

Infamous Bad Languages 2.0

Might begin with mother because I heard you
arguing that, when I was native
to your womb, "indigenous peoples
should pay state taxes for their right to operate
casinos," & on observing
reservation homes you said, "they'd help

themselves by not living
so trashy." I stayed silent

knowing I'd inherited my tongue
that gave me all these poems
so weekly I call you proud
that I've finished a crossword.
But I have to speak, realizing

I plagiarize every word
echoed off your tissue
so I could grasp it, hold
its cadences in my mouth until I learn
that larynx is not just for breath, that tribe

became codified before you
rhymed it, that me filling in
these squares form the boundary
binding us. In my defiance
the entire grid spells resistance
spells love.

*

Capitalism Is Learning to Bleach One's Tongue

Take a roll in sun's circling
contained in threaded bales

nostalgic for that time on the cruise when bandana-women spun straw into cornrows & you said you looked just like my sister, we keep that on the sale rack appropriated from grinning cardboard

"It's beer, mon" a sister will fetch you a key of maps

                              pineapple in the rum-
                                  dwelling synapse

                              vertiginous, a sweet-ass
                                  name for a pirate

once patrolled these shores for proof that the difference between water & capsizing a craft brew is the circumferential floatation of one's equity vest

diamonds on the soles of her Dole bananas

brother of the Chiquita logo rubbing coconut milk all over his skin.

*

I entered my maternal grandmother's house. This was certainly a dream; my parents moved my grandmother, who suffered from Alzheimer's (a mind-rot that eventually killed her), into assisted living when I was in my late 20s. I am now 39.

To my subconscious, the house—a white, two-story structure at the crest of a slight NE Kansas hill—reflected its being unoccupied for several years. While the paint remained unchipped—the wood paneling coated several times to withstand the harsh variances in plains weather—the house did not give off the warmth of a place dwelt in, a home where people lived.

Inside, the floor plan remained the same, though my sleeping mind expanded its rooms to nearly twice their size (SIDENOTE: As a child chasing my cousins through several rooms our mothers & fathers used to call theirs, I thought the house immense; as I grew older, the walls seemed to compress & I wondered how we ever seated 29 people in two rooms for Thanksgiving). Wallpaper peeled away revealing brackish water stains, rotting plaster also. Every step on the now-dull linoleum raised dust.

Enormous webs stretched across framework between hallways & rooms. Intricate in design, the webs demanded study. Their makers were not present. I paused to attend them, every strand from floor to ceiling.

As I scrutinized a particularly complex spiral, its threads began to form into a word, "S-O-U-N-D-I-N-G." A compulsion to reach out, to touch the web as if my fingers would evoke the sign into its signification, came over me. I could not resist. My hand grasped for what I knew it could not contain. The artifice collapsed. Sticky fibers, each the thickness of rubber bands, collared my neck. They began to tighten, to squeeze. I began to perceive the presence of several large ovals dangling in other parts of the web. Unmoving wings protruded from them. Moths. Mummified. Why hadn't I noticed them before?

I struggled for breath (SIDENOTE: I suffer from sleep apnea, so such dreamscape asphyxiations are not uncommon as the hidden and surface worlds merge). I stumbled through the rooms, each one looking increasingly foreign. A study with green shag carpet, a sprawling mahogany desk, a black powder rifle mounted on the wall. A pantry lined with Canopic jars I knew were filled with formaldehyde; in each, an appendage that used to be a thing heard. An unimpressive observatory. A sex dungeon.

With each step, I felt more breath escaping, only I couldn't bring new air in. I ripped at the silk collar, but it only tightened, a spun anaconda sprung from some offense against nature. A kitchen full of broken china. A light slivering beneath a bathroom door.

My fingers pushed against the doorknob. I stumbled & fell inside. A woman stood in front of an antique mirror. She combed out her natural brunette curls with an oyster shell brush. Several tresses covered the marble floor. I interrupted her cutting her hair.

She knelt before me holding old-timey barber shears. Her leg slipped through the crease in her flowered kimono, exposing it full. The pads of her fingers tilted my head forward. She snapped through the web. It fell on top of her unwanted hair. She still held the scissors near my neck's nape.

Outside, I heard a noise building, like thousands of spindled legs rubbing together. Or maybe it was only the small AM/FM radio my grandparents always used to tune in the morning farm report. Whoever tuning it was struggling to pick up a station. The static popped, crackled.

*

FUTURE MUSIC 2.0

Bypasses the ear canal, is static
directly filtered to the auditory cortex

is brought to you by Froot Loops & if
played backwards
does subliminally force worship

of the bygone jewel case. Can't be free,

your listening preferences
having been tracked since when you stared
into the Fisher-Price mobile. The bands
you love become t-shirts

worn under t-shirts
displayed at family zoo outings. Yes,

you knew the song
years before its debut in an iPhone ad.

To think all children
will be born of the consumed
sound clips, will learn to intellectually pirate
silence, seal themselves in

echo chambers intoning
interruptions to the stream.

*

Top 10 List

Always feels confused about her sexual identity
because sometimes it's Channing Tatum's abs
other times ass, sweet hip hop

ass like how can someone even use it
as a serving tray? Top 10 List doesn't even

like that Kanye song. Top 10 List is forever
blue from counting herself
down. Top 10 List cannot complain

when she finds juice cleanses
overrated; Top 10 List knows yoga pants
are so last year. Once, Top 10 List took
a week-long meditation retreat
because her life is forever about organizing
consumption, Top 10 List is tired of finding

post-personhood critiques
within meta-modern narratives. Top 10
List likes when she's juicy, ranking the best

sexual positions among used-to-be
beings involves eating a glazed donut

off her partner's crotch—yes, Top 10 List
is mostly cisgendered. 2 out of ? years
Talenti's sea salt caramel gelato topped 10's

favorite indulgence. When she drives
her preference is torque
based on word-sound, horsepower too
old-fashioned; Top 10 List reinvents herself

annually. All-Decade List
shoves her head in a trashcan
which may be this year's business casual
according to Top 10's fashionable
recycled narrative. Top 10 List looks forward

to tea with Of-The-Century, whose selective
Alzheimer's often marginalizes
what Top 10 is saying. Some nights
Top 10 List gets down

alone watching sports highlights
because she likes abandoning stories. She's used
to cheers & taunts, but sips this year's
best vintage, remembering now
she's memory.

*

Tap List for Ideology™ Craft Beer (Spring 2017)

Privilege Wit (5.0% ABV): After working hard for everything that's come your way, you deserve a crisp, refreshing Americanized European classic. In addition to orange zest & coriander, we've added hints of vanilla & used bready malts that evoke the processed, baked & sliced invention that every great idea compares itself to. There's absolutely no marginalizing this perfect happy-hour beer.

InterPĀLation (5.7% ABV): A perfect pale ale to identify w/, featuring citrusy hop notes & a biscuity body to evoke the 1st time you boldly declared to your friends, "I'm into microbreweries!" Of course, they are too & now you can all toast your discovery. Once this pale ale calls your name, we guarantee you'll always think Ideology™.

E(XXX)ploitation ESB (10.5% ABV): We've taken the ingredients used to brew this traditional British style & pushed it into being our bitch. As a tribute to its production method, this triple ESB is darker in color while retaining a malty sweetness to balance out the trademark bitterness we've pushed 3x the normal limit. This beer will make you feel like a boss.

Repressive Strong Ale (9.5% ABV): Sometimes it takes a firm hand to keep the appetites appeased. We've generously added white sugar to this American-style SA in order to overpower the dark grains & indigenous hops that give this beer its "true character." What results is a potent brew that will keep a stranglehold on your deviant desires.

ISA IPA (7.4% ABV): Subtlety is the main way to describe this refreshing, citrusy beer. While we've consented to brewing America's favorite beer style, we've manufactured a diverse blend of six hops to school your taste buds into accepting our belief that ISA is the best IPA on the market. Try it cask-conditioned to show you're a true connoisseur.

Hegemonic (8.0% ABV) *(available in our unique beer-culture bomber bottles only)*: The beer that made us the craft brewery market-dominating juggernaut we are today. Traditional German doppelbocks feature goats on the label as a testament to their strength, but we've given our goat x-ray vision, GPS to track where you're enjoying the beer & interactive labeling based on your individual drinking preferences. New "cap camera" allows you to take selfies imbibing Hegemonic anywhere!

Commodity Small Batch Series: We take recipes from local homebrewers & give them the chance to use our state-of-the-art equipment to mass produce their ideas for the world. We acquire all rights to recipes & rebranding, but just think of the thrill these small business owners receive seeing their artistic craftwork sold at festivals like Coachella. Our labels are collectible & hand-illustrated by our marketing team as an homage to their industrious vision.

Ideology™ : Proudly Brewing Consent & Conformity for the Post-Person Age & Official Owner-Sponsor of Jerrod E. Bohn's *PULP*.

*

Heart Shaped Box

In middle age, we debate Kurt Cobain
poking around recent arrivals
at the used bookstore. Adjusting
his sweater-sleeves, he tries to avoid

small talking the clerk, to enjoy
his coffee & search
David Foster Wallace books, words
now a sweet musk

on our bedroom floor. Anymore
we never fuck
more than once per week, never
chaff our genitalia raw, but we keep

talking contemporary suicides
let candles blue, green, orange
themselves into night, serene
our vocals' departures into unlit rooms.

*

BACK TO THE FUTURE

Roads have rendered horizons
obsolete; ancient assemblage
of trains vestibules the Western
mind into expansion where we find

a funny car production of the original
time-bending dragster, itself
constructed by Chinese day laborers
manufactured by hand in accessible
seascapes. The idiot
engine is punished for combusting

without oil. Silly horse,
only cardinal directions exist

the 4 corners
lay an arbitrary GPS to 1985

where this year a kid outside
insists chronology is
riding his hover board in a straight line

to the point where sun
both rises & sets, real
coordinates in an imagined California.

*

FOREWORD

In part, *PULP* was inspired by a thoughtful October 2014 essay titled "Poetry, Propaganda, & Political Standards" written by Michael Davis and published for the website *Imaginative Conservative*. Since I don't make a habit of accessing oxymoronic webpages, I can only explain my discovery of Davis's ideas as an act of bibliomancy. But without Davis, this text would only exist in part, Larry Lazarus & "the Voice of my generation" being based on real people I knew growing up. I've fleetingly met some names I mention in this manuscript while others I haven't met at all & I assume they are generally as I depict them (SIDENOTE: & if they aren't, they are in this book & so are, as affected).

To get back to the essay, Davis argues that "as a political medium, poetry is useless." He goes on to suggest (rightly) that readers should not dismiss poets because of their political views so long as they display poetic excellence (SIDENOTE: I deviate in his praise of Eliot as a "matchless poet" as Davis must somehow equate "matchless" with yawn-inducing pretentiousness). Later, Davis asserts (wrongly), "poetry, when not addressing its own medium, will frustrate the reader, the writer, and the poem itself." Davis's latter statement seems to suggest that all poetry is metapoetry & that the only suitable poetic topic is poetry itself. What Davis overlooks—& to which I owe enormous gratitude for rounding out our hero, Larry Lazarus—is that frustration can have enormous subversive power & may well be indispensable as a political & ethical dimension of poetry (SIDENOTE: I would venture to guess, given Davis's conservatism, that "frustration" is what leads him to dismiss Ginsberg's "Howl" as "bourgeoisie degeneracy").

Patricia Lockwood is a terrific example of a poet who uses frustration progressively. In her poem "Rape Joke" Lockwood frustrates reader anticipation of discovering humor through its reformulations of invitations to laugh at rape; moreover, she frustrates by her grounded ambiguity, falsely suggesting that readers might declare—once & for all—a rape joke to be appropriate or inappropriate. Through this frustration, readers are forced to turn inward & examine their own attitudes, to peer at their own comedy, the justice of it.

Davis dismisses that frustration can bring about micro or macro revolution (I'm certain because of his fear), that when one side is "frustrated" by another's insensitivity, to give those feelings voice at the risk of "frustrating" the offender might open the door to meaningful dialogue. Additionally, Davis seems to champion a poetics of craft alone, where the value of a poem is measured purely by its carefully executed manipulation of formal techniques, including rhythms & meters that no one knows the names of anyway (SIDENOTE: in typical conservative fashion, this allows readers to ignore the importance of Claudia Rankine's *Citizen* because its prose poem structure & use of the readerly "you" isn't particularly surprising or "matchless").

What Davis forgets is emotion, the same emotional force that led Shelley to declare that "poets are the legislators of the world." Poetry matters because it invites the reader into a dialogue where the world is named & necessitates renaming again & again. Frustration is another way of disrupting narrative forces that author the world through lenses of power (SIDENOTE: it is little wonder that Davis writes for a conservative publication & that Davis observes that conservative poets are not persecuted for their political views because conservatives often comprise the repressive & ideological apparatuses that create a marginalizing system).

I'm not advocating a poetics of shock value or frustration for frustration's sake (or even suggesting that frustration is the sole purpose of the poem, as there are numerous possibilities); like Davis, I would dismiss a poem that I modally cannot accept as a poem regardless of its political message. Rather, I believe poetry should proceed with the intention of establishing a mutually participatory space of dialectic-linguistic encounter between two persons.

Lockwood's poem uses words to move through space & become action. In their wake, an obliteration. A Freeing. Poetry is the always failed attempt to establish a just world which may result in liberation through renaming one dialogue at a time.

*

Larry Lazarus reigns in to the last American
drive-in. He's here-to-see
the "voice" narrating his live action
GoBots movie:

Free of CGI, the GoBots movie reunites *Ironic MetaLove Narrative's* Larry Lazarus & Ariana as androgynous vehicles that transform into gendered, assembly-line laborers that manufacture post-persons in an egalitarian dystopia. Having just abolished chattel slavery, the Apparatus operates massive factories that churn out 99% of the world's workforce. The Apparatus is governed by wealthy, "plain, unassorted white males" who ride evil, mutant-robot motorcycles. They recognize each other by their leather jackets & their trump card patches. They control through the dissemination of

this pulp, this metapoetry, this
scripture, this speaking for collective

Larry saw etched into an airport urinal

looking down,

"Slaves became willing participants because they accepted slavery as their identity"—the "Voice," previously cited. Amendment: "accepted" through "coercion & some unknowingly." A football star (Colin Kaepernick in his first acting role) discovers he can affect change & enlists the help of Ariana (as BugBite) & Larry Lazarus (as Road Ranger) to rebel against the Apparatus. Wearing repurposed electronics boxes instead of metallic body armor, BugBite & Road Ranger heroically battle the monstrous Trumpies as the noble athlete must discourse against The Apparatus's Narrative in an attempt to liberate the 99% to personhood

emerging into full light
sound of flickering fires

Larry is his hand, groping
rockwall, feels again

his finger's sum.

About the Author

Jerrod E. Bohn's poetry and nonfiction have appeared in numerous journals, and he is also the author of the book *Animal Histories* (Unsolicited Press 2017). A graduate of Colorado State University's MFA program, Jerrod currently resides in Seattle, WA where he teaches English and yoga. When not reading and writing, he enjoys cooking, craft breweries, and anything outdoors.

About the Press

Unsolicited Press was founded in 2012 by writers and editors who had grown tired of the standard publishing practices (particularly in how writers were over-looked). The press is currently based in Portland, Oregon and published exemplary fiction, nonfiction, and poetry. Learn more at www.unsolicitedpress.com.

www.ingramcontent.com/pod-product-compliance
Lightning Source LLC
Chambersburg PA
CBHW052055110526
44591CB00013B/2216